GARDENS
of NEW
ORLEANS

GARDENS of NEW ORLEANS

EXQUISITE EXCESS

Jeannette Hardy *and* Lake Douglas

Photographs by Richard Sexton

CHRONICLE BOOKS

SAN FRANCISCO

Library of Congress Cataloging-in-Publication Data:
Douglas, Lake, 1949–
    Gardens of New Orleans: Exquisite Excess /
    by Lake Douglas and Jeannette Hardy ;
    photographs by Richard Sexton.
    208 p.   25 x 25 cm.
    Includes bibliographical references (p. 203).
    ISBN 0-8118-2421-7
    1. Gardens—Louisiana—New Orleans. 2. Parks—
    Louisiana—New Orleans. I. Hardy, Jeannette,
    1943–   II. Title.
    SB466.U65 N664 2001
    712'.09763'35—dc21   00-43013

Printed in China

Distributed in Canada by Raincoast Books
9050 Shaughnessy Street
Vancouver, British Columbia V6P 6E5

10 9 8 7 6 5 4 3 2 1

Chronicle Books LLC
85 Second Street
San Francisco, California 94105

www.chroniclebooks.com

COVER

Sumptuous tropicals and natives billow out from the gallery of Ralph and Doris Cadow's Royal Street townhouse, transforming it into a lush urban bower.

PAGE 2

Picked at the end of a dry summer and fall, a clump of green bananas is stored on the porch at the home of Malcolm and Alicia Heard.

PAGE 6

Showy and fragrant angel's trumpets cascade over lush plantings of crinums and other natives in the Heards' Bywater garden.

PAGES 10–11

A swamp scene, thirty minutes away from downtown New Orleans, shows the region's natural landscape much as early settlers must have encountered it. Surrounding the blooming native Louisiana iris (there are four native species, Iris fulva, brevicaulis, nelsonii, and giganticaerulea) are plants native to the swamp. Dwarf palmetto covers the marshy ground plane, and overhead are swamp red maples, bald cypress, and tupelo gum trees.

*Dedicated to
the gardeners
of New Orleans,
past and present*

Contents

Introduction

For every one of the mansions, cottages, shotguns, and bungalows that fill the refined and crusty neighborhoods of New Orleans, there is some kind of garden—at the very least a spontaneous one, courtesy of the lush subtropical climate that sprouts things without asking permission. Some of them are magnificently tended, some are in a dreamy state of dilapidation, and lots of them are somewhere in between. But no matter what their condition, like other visual treats in the city, the gardens reflect layers that only time and a diverse population can provide.

Originally founded on the graceful French and Spanish traditions of landscaping, the gardens of New Orleans today represent a lavish hodgepodge. There are plenty of native live oaks and magnolias, to be sure. And there are plenty of time-honored exotics, such as camellias and gardenias. But proud additions from other cultures and sensibilities have brought a gusto unrivaled in most American cities. So, cheek by jowl with the old standbys, you'll find crinums from Africa, salvias from Mexico, lantanas from the Mediterranean, gingers from the Caribbean, lemon grass from Vietnam, and bamboos from China and Japan.

Because of these and other blessings, New Orleans is a place of unending surprise. It's there on the stage of everyday life, where a homebrew of people and art collide to produce exotic pageantry—rarefied music from jazz to rap, inventive food from red beans to redfish, architecture from colonial to contemporary.

And the range is just as rich in the world of plants and gardens.

Reared on a history that began with primordial swamplands simmered in subtropical temperatures, the gardens, like the city's other art forms, have gathered stature with each wave of newcomers.

The French brought knowledge about horticulture and design from their native soil, allowing the city's gardens to expand and evolve on the framework of their sturdy tradition. The Spanish, along with the French, introduced the notion of enclosed courtyards and patios, as well as balconies and galleries. Africans brought exotic plants and know-how from their homeland; Germans brought their state-of-the-art skills. And after the Louisiana Purchase, the tenets of English garden style came to town, compliments of the *Americains,* as they were known in New Orleans. And so it went, layer after layer.

If the gardens of New Orleans are simply part of everyday life to hometowners, they have always made a powerful impression on visitors. Antoine Simon Le Page de Pratz, an eighteenth-century explorer who landed here, described the startling array of crops, fruit trees, shrubs, creeping plants, and "excrescences" he found in the region. With amazing foresight for 1819, architect Benjamin Henry Latrobe reported that New Orleans might be one of the "most delightful abodes of affluence & elegance in the world were it not for the muskitoes." And Frederick Law Olmsted, father of

Lakeshore Fishing Village, circa 1870, by Marshall J. Smith Jr. (1854–1923), captures the natural landscape around Lake Pontchartrain. Active in the 1870s and early 1880s, Smith was instrumental in the emerging art scene in late-nineteenth-century New Orleans. (The Roger Ogden Museum of Southern Art, University of New Orleans)

American landscape architecture, writing in the 1850s, noted the similarity between plants blooming in Jackson Square and those he had seen in the south of France.

From these accounts and others, we can reconstruct the evolution of the city's landscape heritage and see how its gardens reflect the past while accommodating the present. Still very much alive is the tradition of garden enclosures, often linked to the house by transitional spaces such as courtyards or balconies or porches.

For those with an inclination to savor them, memorable images and sensual impressions are everywhere. Canopies of live oaks transform ordinary streets into extravagant tunnels; night-blooming jasmine lends gentle fragrance to sweltering summer evenings; choruses of frogs drown out noise from cars and sirens and other man-made urban intrusions.

As for the landscapes themselves, some are easier than others to experience. The great public parks—Audubon Park and City Park—are there for everyone to explore, as are the smaller neighborhood green spaces and the grand boulevards. The private gardens, coaxed and tended and cherished by everyone from dig-in-the-dirt amateurs to professional impresarios, are harder to know. What follows, with an explanation of their roots and influences, are their stories.

—JEANNETTE HARDY AND LAKE DOUGLAS

A Brief History

*T*HE NEW WORLD'S SOUTHERN COAST ATTRACTED SETTLERS eager to take advantage of the land's agreeable climate and its promise of economic success. In the early eighteenth century, the French established an outpost, La Nouvelle Orléans, in a wide crescent bend of the Mississippi River. From the many Native Americans living in the Lower Mississippi River region— the Houma, Tunica, Chitimacha, Biloxi, Coushatta, and Pascagoula tribes—the early French settlers learned how to survive in the new colony. To them, this part of the New World and its inhabitants were alien and exotic. The wide river with stands of cypress trees and swamps teeming with peculiar wildlife was surely a spectacular sight. ❈ At the Jean Lafitte National Historical Park and Preserve, thirty minutes from today's downtown New Orleans, visitors exploring the wooden boardwalks and foot trails get a taste of what those early settlers experienced. Alligators glide slowly through murky waters, and snakes sun themselves on fallen trees. Snow white egrets and slate blue herons glide effortlessly across the sky. Armadillos scurry through the undergrowth, and large black spiders spin webs that span distances of several feet, forming lacy patterns that hold the morning dew and catch passing insects. Clouds of buzzing insects are always in the air, and graceful mosquito hawks dart from branch to branch. The ground is wet and mucky or, at a slightly higher elevation, dry and covered with a thick blanket of leaves. The swamp is redolent of

A 1755 map shows an extraordinary inventory of colonial structures and parterre gardens. Most of the gardens and structures were likely figments of the cartographer's imagination. (The Historic New Orleans Collection, 1939.8)

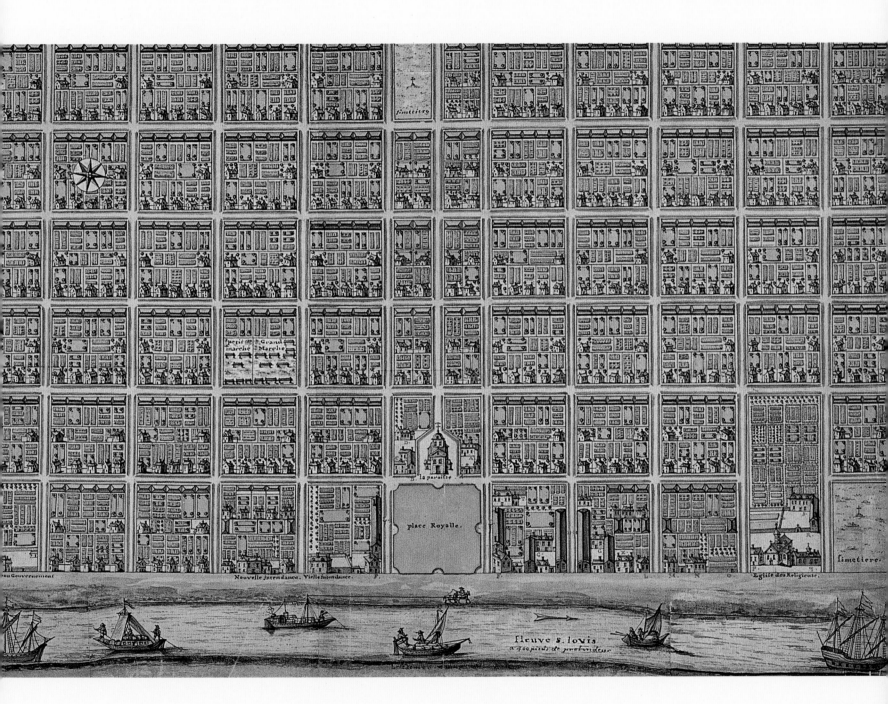

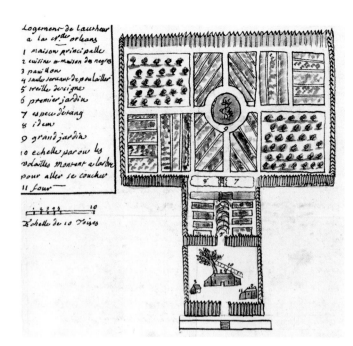

An early map, circa 1730, drawn by François Benjamin Dumont de Montigny depicts early settlers' structures and utilitarian gardens, surrounded by a wooden stockade. According to the map's key, the ladder in the tree (#10) behind the main structure allows chickens to "get up into the tree to roost." (Newberry Library, Chicago, Illinois)

accumulated rot and decay, yet its thick odor is full of fertile promise.

Against this backdrop, early settlers went about the business of building a frontier outpost, following military models and prototypes from their homelands. Periodic storms and fires devastated this early settlement throughout the eighteenth century, yet residents continued to rebuild. With each new structure, this small community—the part of New Orleans now known as the Vieux Carré, or French Quarter—became less reliant on foreign models, and its urban form more expressive of local conditions.

Early maps of the colony show an array of domestic garden spaces laid into rectangular or square plots, with features ranging from shrubbery at the corners of rectangular plots to intricate *parterre de broderie,* or planting beds with plants used in embroidery-like patterns. Were the elaborate gardens shown in early maps all here? Probably not, neither in the quantity nor in the refinement shown. More likely, what gardens did exist in this frontier outpost contained vegetables rather than decorative *parterres.*

The Ursuline Convent had one of the earliest gardens. Dating from the late 1720s when the Sisters of St. Ursula came from France, this garden grew herbs and plants for the convent's residents, hospital, and orphanage. Early officials reported on the medicinal virtues of native plants, yet there was little interest in growing native plant materials here; instead, they depended on plants sent from France.

Few early French settlers had agricultural skills or interest in acquiring them. Native Americans, African slaves, and German and Swiss immigrants filled this vacuum of farming expertise. German farmers, who were particularly industrious, became notable providers of produce grown on small farms with narrow plots facing the river. Initially, these farmers sold their products in the nearby community; by mid-century, they grew sufficient amounts to export.

By the second half of the eighteenth century, agricultural settlements in outlying regions were prosperous plantations producing rice, indigo, and sugarcane. These large-scale operations required field hands brought from Africa and the Caribbean for their experience in growing these crops.

Some of these slaves developed a parallel, small-scale agricultural economy. An exemption from forced work on weekends and religious holidays gave them free time to work their own gardens and sell their produce in public marketplaces and squares and from carts in the streets. These free-market practices continued through the nineteenth century. Even today there are vegetable vendors who sell on street corners or maintain regular routes through neighborhoods, calling out their inventory with lyrical chants: "I got your fresh strawberries; I got your Creole tomatoes; I got nice turnips. . . ."

Little of the colonial city and certainly no gardens from this period survive. Yet as visitors

UNDER MY WINGS EVERY THING PROSPERS

roam the city, they can see vestiges from colonial times that have helped create today's distinctive fabric: buildings, often joined by common walls, faced street-front property lines; stables, small vegetable plots, wash areas, chicken coops, and service areas for other necessary household activities were in rear courtyards and side yards; when vegetable and fruit gardens existed, they were in rectangular beds that facilitated cultivation.

When the United States purchased the Louisiana Territory from France in 1803, New Orleans was a growing center of commerce and an enclave of European and Creole influences, but it was not necessarily a community of culture and refinement. Illiteracy was common, as was civil strife caused by the diverse natures of local residents. According to travelers' accounts,

lush vegetation surrounded the town along the Mississippi River, and gardens were orderly and utilitarian. Newspaper advertisements from the mid-1820s document the availability of specific plants and indicate an expanding trade in horticultural goods and services.

In early 1828, a man advertised his services as a "gardener and florist planter, and cutter of trees and vines." He touted experience based on having studied "under the most celebrated master gardeners of Europe" and boasted of "perfect knowledge of the cultivation of vegetables both indigenous and exotic"— quite a qualified professional. What is more important, though, is evidence of a direct link between European garden practices and New Orleans gardens.

Itinerant engineer and artist John L. Boqueta de Woiseri made this aquatint with added watercolor. A View of New Orleans, one of the earliest urban views of an American city, shows New Orleans in 1803, the year of the Louisiana Purchase. Looking upriver, it shows in the foreground a portion of the garden of Bernard X. P. de Marigny's plantation. The spires of St. Louis Cathedral are right of center, and trees are planted on the Mississippi River's levee. (The Historic New Orleans Collection, 1958.42)

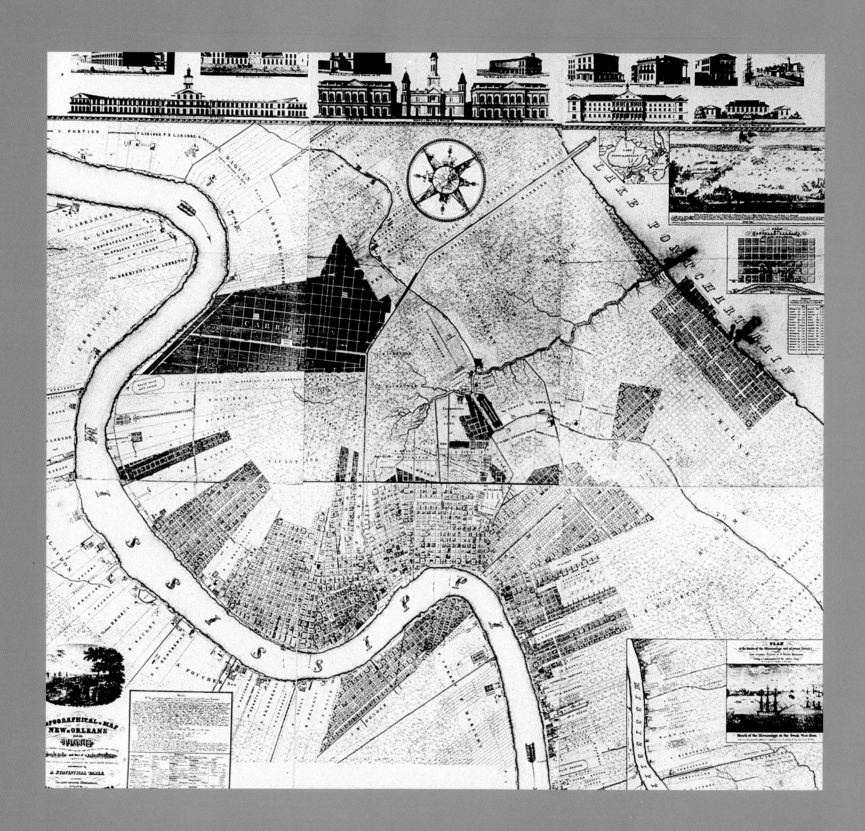

As the city grew, new neighborhoods provided new opportunities for gardens. A remarkably detailed map from 1834 (left) shows the developed parts of the city and locations of buildings as well as public squares, domestic gardens, and street tree plantings along major avenues.

One of America's first garden books is J. F. Lelievre's *Nouveau Jardinier de la Louisiane,* published in New Orleans in 1838. It is a small book (about four and one-half inches by six and one-half inches), and though much of its text is general in scope, it has specific references to the soils, weather, and native plants of "lower Louisiana." The guide is valuable for local garden historians because it includes lists of vegetables and flowering plants—from garlic, celery, and sweet pepper to four o'clock, marigold, and hydrangea—and confirms the availability of technical garden resources.

Nationally circulated magazines established in the early nineteenth century soon became a popular means of mass communication. Articles on New Orleans gardens provide detailed, yet conflicting, information about local gardening in the 1840s.

One article in *The Magazine of Horticulture,* by J. W. Paulsen, described the garden of C. L. Bell. "I found the weather, at my arrival, very warm and perfectly delightful—a beautiful Italian sky, and almost no wind," Paulsen wrote. "Mr. Bell's garden presented to me very much the appearance of a vast conservatory, studded with West Indian plants, growing in the greatest profusion. Great numbers of tree-like oleanders, eugenias, jasmines, pomegranates, and myrtles, with their dark, somber foliage, gave a stateliness and grandeur to the scenery, while their blossoms spread a delicious fragrance around, and their branches afford shelter to the mocking-bird. The contrast of these dark evergreens with beds of bright and dazzling flowers beneath, proved to my northern eyes pleasing and unique in the extreme." This and another account by a writer from Baton Rouge suggested that, as elsewhere in the country, gardens were increasingly used as showcases for plants.

A contradictory view, "Random Notes on Southern Horticulture," appeared in the May 1851 edition of *The Horticulturist.* The author, Sylvanus, observed that "though nature has done much to adorn the scene, art has done little or nothing . . . You would be astonished at the few varieties of trees and shrubs, and flowers, you would meet with" and "there is not much true horticultural taste here, or much knowledge of trees and shrubs," given that "there are no large nurseries from which trees and shrubs may be seen and procured." In this observer's view, "Landscape Gardening [in New Orleans] is half a century behind the age."

Despite Sylvanus's criticisms, the city's gardeners clearly had access to horticultural information and supplies. By midcentury, New Orleans was one of America's largest cities and a center of commerce and fashion for the southern United States. Regular trade connected New Orleans with other major cities in the United States and Europe, introducing new plants as well as contemporary ideas about gardening.

Norman's Southern Agricultural Almanac For 1847, published in New Orleans, lists over 50 agricultural, horticultural, and farming manuals or journals for sale (many published in other

American or European cities) and contains local merchants' advertisements for plants, tools, and equipment. For several years, the almanac was edited by Thomas Affleck, a native of Scotland who established a successful nursery outside of Natchez, Mississippi, and maintained a regular horticultural trade, via riverboat, in the 1850s between Natchez and his numerous clients in New Orleans. Several plant merchants had been doing business in New Orleans since the 1820s and 1830s, and by the end of the 1850s, at least one large nursery offered plants and horticultural advice to its customers. The catalog from John M. Nelson's Magnolia Nursery gives practical gardening advice and a detailed listing of available plants, notably fruit trees, evergreen and deciduous trees and shrubs, 18 varieties of camellias, and 160 varieties of roses. Nelson notes in his catalog that only fruits "well adapted to the soil and climate of the South" are listed, and "new varieties are added to the catalogue as soon as they are proved suitable to the climate."

By midcentury, the city had several types of domestic architecture—the plantation or farmhouse, the single or double Creole cottage, and the townhouse, often in Italianate and Greek Revival styles. Single and double shotgun cottages came later in the century as the major house type for the city's working classes. Many examples of these structures are shown in New Orleans Notarial Archives drawings, made by accomplished surveyors and artists when properties were sold from the early 1800s through the early 1900s. Some drawings include garden plans and elevations that are lush and detailed, with trees (weeping willow, cherry laurel, and chinaberry), shrubs (banana, althea, and camel-

lia), and vines (rose and ivy). Though these drawings record conditions at the time properties changed hands, general garden types can often be connected with specific architectural styles. Utilitarian gardens are associated with farmhouses and cottages or shotgun houses on smaller lots in working-class neighborhoods, while elaborate ornamental gardens often accompanied grander Greek Revival houses on more spacious lots in affluent areas.

Plantations and farmhouses, found usually in rural areas surrounding the community, were small or large, simple or grand. Their gardens were often organized into linear borders or rectangular beds, largely for function and efficiency of production rather than for ornamental purposes. The beds probably grew common ingredients used in local cuisine, such as tomato, okra, pepper, green onion, garlic, celery, and eggplant. Larger properties might have an orchard—citrus, plum, and fig are common in written sources—and trellises held vines such as mirleton (vegetable pear) and native grapes (muscadine and scuppernong). The expanding city eventually absorbed farmhouse and plantation properties, and large tracts were divided into smaller lots for new neighborhoods. Where they still exist, farmhouses often occupy sites larger than those of other house types, and owners often use these spaces for vegetable gardens, expanses of lawn, or outdoor living areas.

Simple and straightforward, Creole cottages were common throughout the community. Like farmhouses, they vary from very simple structures on small plots in working-class neighborhoods to grand, raised center-hall versions lining major streets. For simple homes, gardens were

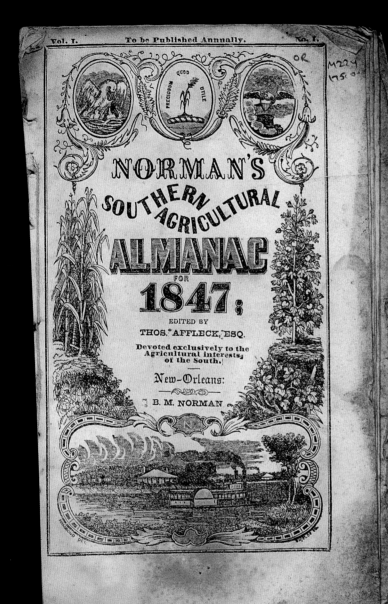

Vol. I.   To be Published Annually.   No. I.

OR
M224
175.00

NORMAN'S
SOUTHERN AGRICULTURAL
ALMANAC
FOR
1847;

EDITED BY
THOS. AFFLECK, ESQ.

Devoted exclusively to the
Agricultural interests
of the South.

New-Orleans:

B. M. NORMAN

PRECIOSUM QUOD UTILE

CATALOGUE
OF
FRUIT, SHADE AND ORNAMENTAL TREES,
EVERGREENS, ROSES,
AND
MISCELLANEOUS PLANTS,
CULTIVATED AND FOR SALE BY
JOHN M. NELSON,
At the Magnolia Nurseries,
METAIRIE RIDGE, AND
AT HIS PLANT DEPOT,
Corner of Camp street and Lafayette Square,
NEW ORLEANS.

N. B.—Plants of every description furnished from the Magnolia
Nurseries, GUARANTEED FREE OF COCO.

PRINTED AT THE OFFICE OF THE TRUE DELTA, 18 ST. CHARLES ST.
1859.

PERSPECTIVE FRONT VIEW

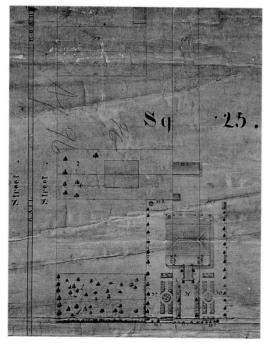

Sq. 25.

This farmhouse illustration, dated 1835, shows a structure from the late eighteenth or early nineteenth century. Geometric beds lie between the house and the street, behind a hedge and fence. Off to one side is a yard with scattered trees or shrubs, a parcel that could have been added later to the property. (Plan Book 29, Folio 28; 1835; New Orleans Notarial Archives)

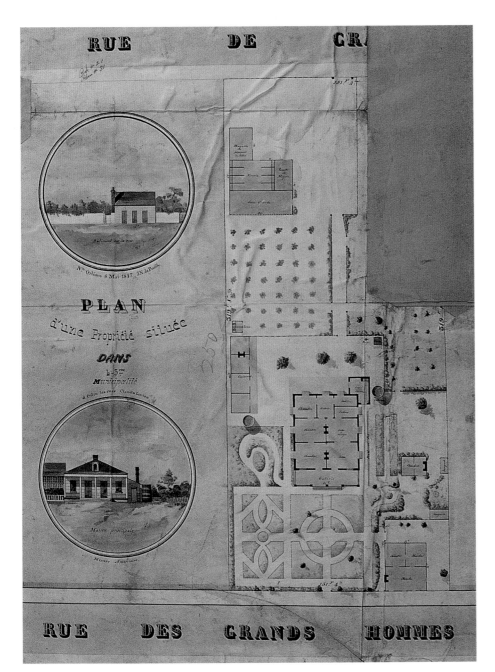

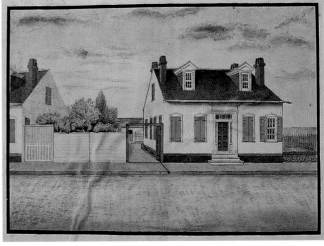

Dating from 1847, this plan shows an elaborate garden with fanciful beds, an orchard, and outbuildings. Plots appear to have been added to the property over time, creating a large complex of buildings and outdoor spaces. (Plan Book 21, Folio 31; 1847; New Orleans Notarial Archives)

This central hall cottage, with steps directly on the sidewalk, has a long, narrow planting bed on the side, separated from the structure by an alleyway. (Plan Book 11, Folio 38; 1845; New Orleans Notarial Archives) typically at the side or rear, a pattern that continues today. Archival drawings show garden beds in geometric shapes. Larger properties had more elaborate gardens, often with arbors and orchards. Today's visitor will find gardens around Creole cottages in many versions, ranging from simple lawns with a few shrubs to yards with imaginative plantings. They reflect interior uses of the house, and although often limited in space, they offer many options for the creative gardener.

By far the most prevalent house type was the shotgun, built on long, narrow lots and containing a series of square or rectangular rooms lined up one behind the other. There is no interior hallway, but a side gallery sometimes serves as an exterior hallway. Shotguns were single-family homes or side-by-side structures—a double shotgun—that served as two-family dwellings. Often directly on the sidewalk, they occupied most of the property's width, leaving little, if any, room for front or side gardens. When garden plans occur, they often resembled those of Creole cottages: small, long rectangular beds, usually raised slightly to accommodate drainage. These were working-class homes, and their gardens, if any, were organized for limited production rather than ornament. Many examples of shotgun houses remain from the late nineteenth and early twentieth centuries; like cottages, they offer today's owners challenging garden opportunities because of their limited spaces.

Located in the city's central, urbanized areas, townhouses were usually adjacent to sidewalks, sometimes with carriageways that allowed access from the street to courtyards or rear service yards. Paved in flagstone or brick, these courtyards were often visible from the street through carriageway gates. Late nineteenth- and early twentieth-century accounts of courtyards described them as mysterious places of romance and lush vegetation. These exterior spaces, however, were more commonly functional. Courtyards provided light and air for their surrounding structures. They were also the locations for domestic activities not contained in the house—such as the privy; garbage dump; cistern for capturing water; spaces for a horse, pets, or chickens; laundry; and other outbuildings. This left little space for ornamental gardening. Any planting beds were adjacent to the kitchen and servants' quarters, suggesting uses related to cooking or running the house. Only when functional activities were relocated off-site did enclosed courtyard spaces become more ornamental in character. Larger nineteenth-century townhouses of wealthier owners often had both functional and ornamental areas; however, widespread uses of balconies and courtyards for ornamental gardens are relatively modern developments.

Greek Revival houses usually were on larger lots in suburban neighborhoods that developed from the 1830s onward. Set back from the street, these detached structures allowed for extensive front, side, and rear gardens. Ornamental gardens in the front and side yards were often exuberantly planted with many different varieties of plants. Vegetable gardens or small orchards were in the rear.

Unlike the close-knit fabric of the eighteenth-century French Quarter, neighborhoods that developed by the mid-nineteenth century in other parts of the city featured freestanding structures set in large rectangular lots. The best example is the Garden District, a neighborhood

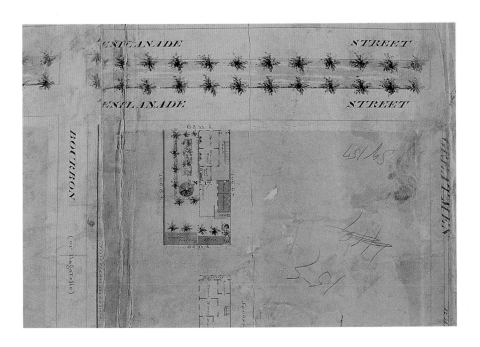

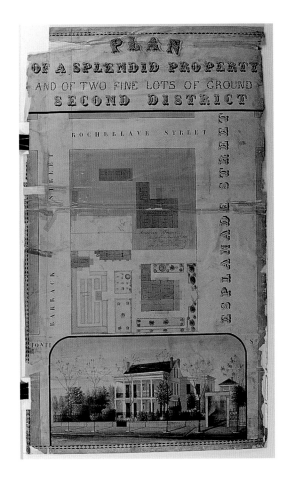

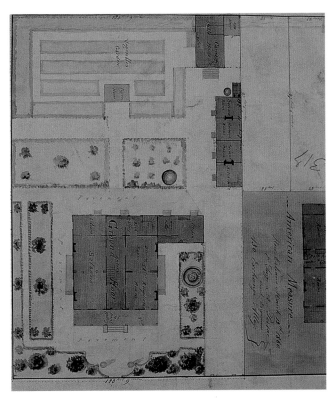

An urban scene, circa 1858, at the intersection of Polymnia Street and Felicity Street. Structures were built directly on sidewalk property lines, with little space for front gardens. Streets were unpaved, with deep gutters for rain runoff and urban debris. (The Historic New Orleans Collection. 1982.32.14)

with grand houses and often elaborate gardens. Once part of the Livaudais plantation, this tract—including the adjacent neighborhood known as the Irish Channel—was purchased by American land speculators in the early 1830s. After a grid system of streets was established, the subdivision was incorporated into a suburban community. This scheme was designed to facilitate the construction of large, detached "villas" in garden settings, in contrast to the narrow lots of older neighborhoods.

The area closest to the Mississippi River soon filled with dock activities, warehouses, slaughterhouses, and small frame houses for workers, mostly of Irish and German descent; this working-class neighborhood soon became known as the Irish Channel. But property closer

to St. Charles Avenue, where one of America's first public transit lines developed, became a fashionable garden suburb as American merchants and bankers moved into the city.

By the late 1840s and early 1850s, the city's economic, business, political, and social communities were governed by residents of Anglo-American heritage, rather than those of Creole or French backgrounds. Many of them lived in the Garden District, and they preferred large Greek Revival and Italianate architectural styles surrounded by spacious gardens. Large lot sizes, increased wealth, and available immigrant labor enabled the wealthy to build houses with extensive areas of shrubs, blooming plants, and trees, now available from local nurseries or shipped from sources in the Northeast or Europe.

Regardless of location, midcentury gardens often featured purely ornamental planting beds, complex and crowded with contrasting textures, colors, and shapes and embellished with cast-iron fences, benches, planters, and fountains, many from local suppliers. Plants included both natives and exotics introduced from Central America and the Orient. Crape myrtle, azalea, camellia, althea, and other members of the hibiscus family were common, as were rose, oleander, and jasmine. According to one written source, gardens here were "a tolerable display of Flora's beauties" that delighted mid-nineteenth-century visitors as much then as they please the tourists of today.

As the Civil War approached, New Orleans was a bustling city. Its population was four times that of any other southern city and equaled that of Cincinnati, St. Louis, Baltimore, and Boston. Developments spread out from the French Quarter in all directions, creating neighborhoods known today as Mid-City, Esplanade Ridge, Algiers, Bywater, and the Faubourgs Marigny, St. John, and Tremé. Though each was different, they shared many architectural and horticultural elements. New Orleans was the most cosmopolitan city in the South, and its gardens reflected the community's multicultural heritage, its access to international markets, and residents' interest in contemporary styles.

In contrast to domestic gardens, urban conditions were grim. Some streets had plantings of trees, but most remained unpaved until the end of the century. Sidewalks were often dirt, covered with wooden planks; sometimes they were paved with brick or flagstone. Property drained directly into open ditches bordering the streets, causing frequent flooding. Residents continued to leave the city in the summer to avoid the heat and disagreeable conditions.

Improvements were slow to come after the Civil War because New Orleans had a relatively small tax base and a high municipal debt. Political corruption ran rampant, prompting voters to reject new taxes for civic improvements. There was little political incentive, civic foresight, or public will to change the status quo.

Several small public parks were scattered about the city—Jackson Square in the Vieux Carré, Washington Square in Marigny, Lafayette Square in the American sector, and Annunciation and Coliseum Square in the Lower Garden District—but no initiatives were introduced to build large-scale parks until the century's end. Individual donors or associations of concerned citizens generally funded nineteenth-century improvements to park spaces. This practice continues today as neighborhood associations and volunteer organizations actively support individual components of the city's green space network.

Seeking to demonstrate that New Orleans had recovered from the Civil War and Reconstruction and to advertise the city's improved port, business and civic leaders mounted the World's Industrial and Cotton Centennial Exposition in 1884–1885. Like its predecessor in Philadelphia (1876) and its successor in Chicago (1893), the New Orleans world's fair had a significant impact on the local community. It displayed new inventions such as the electric light and influenced public awareness of open spaces and horticulture.

An interior view of Horticulture Hall from the World's Industrial and Cotton Centennial Exposition of 1884–1885 by local commercial photographer George F. Mugnier. The fair's exhibits and horticultural displays introduced new plants and garden features to local residents. The grounds on which the event was held subsequently became Audubon Park. (Louisiana State Museum)

The fair occupied a large tract that had been a sugar plantation up the Mississippi River from the city center. One of the major buildings was Horticulture Hall, modeled after Joseph Paxton's Crystal Palace of 1851 in London. It had exotic tropical plants, horticultural displays, animals (the city's first zoo), and basins with goldfish and floating water hyacinth, a plant that escaped cultivation into local swamps. Features set trends in planting and garden furnishings

Since early colonial times, Native Americans and European settlers sold agricultural goods, meat, and fish at local public markets. This view of the French Market, the city's first public market and one of the country's oldest public markets still in operation, dates from 1880–1890.
(Louisiana State Museum)

and soon became established in local public and private gardens.

The city continued to expand in the late nineteenth century as new immigrants arrived. By century's end, immigrants from southern Italy had gradually taken over the roles of greengrocer and truck farmer. Nevertheless German horticultural businesses, such as seed stores, supply houses, florists, and gardeners, established earlier in the century, remained and

flourished. A few of these enterprises still exist today as reminders of these important horticultural influences in the community.

As the city grew and its economy expanded, gardens became important to middle-class residents who sought new horticultural goods and services. Florists also provided garden design, installation, and maintenance services. Local foundries offered a variety of garden cast-iron furnishings: ornamental animals; fountains

No. 7

HINDERER'S
IRON FENCE WORKS
MANUFACTURER OF
Ornamental Iron Vases,
1112-1118 Camp St., NEW ORLEANS, LA.

The following Styles of Vases will be found the most Ornamental, Practical and most desirable Vases for the use in Public Parks, Gardens, Lawns and Cemeteries. This is one of our Specialties on which we can make you astonishing LOW PRICES. Convince yourself by giving us a call or write for prices. All goods in stock for immediate delivery.

ASK FOR SPECIAL CATALOGUE OF LAWN FURNITURE AND DRINKING FOUNTAINS.

ASK FOR SPECIAL FENCE CATALOGUE.

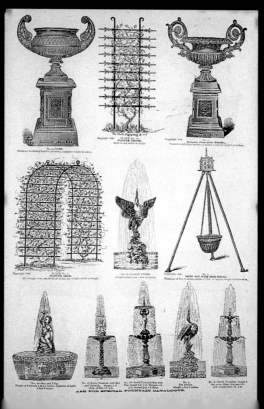

ASK FOR SPECIAL FOUNTAIN CATALOGUE.

OPPOSITE

*Hinderer's Iron Works,
a local firm, produced iron
furniture, fences, fountains,
and various garden features
for residential gardens, public
parks, and cemeteries. Fence
components from this late
nineteenth-century catalog
are still visible throughout
the city.* (Author's Collection)

RIGHT

*Images of the French Quarter,
such as this one circa 1930
by photographer Frances
B. Johnston, show that courtyard spaces were used more
for service functions such as
laundry and other necessities
of high-density living. Later
when these functions were
moved either inside or elsewhere in the community
and interest awakened in
architectural preservation,
the secluded spaces were
planted and enjoyed as gardens.*
(Tulane University, Southeast
Architecture Archive; Ray
Thompson collection)

and water basins; urns and vases; seats and benches; arbors and trellises; and fences and gates. By century's end, gardens had changed from simple spaces with minimal plantings to elaborate designs stocked with both plants and man-made objects.

At the end of the twentieth century's first decade, New Orleans had begun to improve its urban amenities and recover its national position of economic prominence. There were two large public parks, one with a new art museum. Storm drainage systems drained newly paved streets, and streetcar lines laced the community together, providing residents access to distant attractions. Plantings of live oaks, now matured, lined major streets.

A growing interest in the city's historic architecture led to pioneering preservation legislation in the 1920s for the French Quarter. Architects and artists documented older structures and helped locals preserve and transform high-density tenements back to their original uses as single-family homes. Interior courtyards that had, for many years, been devoted to utilitarian functions became outdoor rooms with spaces for lush plantings. Over time, fountains, swimming pools, and patios replaced vegetable plots, chicken coops, and laundry yards. Balconies and galleries became elevated gardens for those who lived in second- and third-floor apartments.

Few landscape architects practiced in the city in the first half of the twentieth century. John Charles Olmsted, working on Audubon Park, and Ellen Biddle Shipman, designing Longue Vue, commuted from the East Coast. Local landscape architect William Wiedorn worked on projects in City Park, but most residential gardens were the creations of experienced garden club members or architects such as Richard Koch. As elsewhere in America, much of the enthusiasm for gardens, garden history, and public parks came from women interested in domestic activities and community projects.

World War II temporarily halted most urban development, but the 1950s and 1960s, fueled by postwar prosperity, saw major changes in the city's form. Families of returning veterans created a demand for new housing. Locals left older neighborhoods for new subdivisions built along the lakefront and in adjacent Jefferson

Parish. Older inner-city neighborhoods declined as newer automobile-oriented suburbs prospered. Houses for single families were detached and often ranch style, with few concessions to local building traditions or historical styles. Instead, they had outdoor patios that conformed to the ideas of exterior design and modern lifestyles emerging from postwar California.

As a profession, landscape architecture became visible in New Orleans only when professionals opened offices in the 1960s. Most local landscape architects graduated from the Louisiana State University program in nearby Baton Rouge, a curriculum that emphasized physical design, local plant materials, and travel to study important urban and landscape developments throughout the country. New graduates introduced concepts to local projects that corresponded with national and international trends in planting, spatial design, and exterior activities.

For the first time in its history, the city hired a landscape architect for its Parks and Parkway Department in the early 1970s. As federal funding became available for urban amenities, design professionals began to renovate older parks and create new spaces—such as vest-pocket parks and streetscape improvements—under the city's direction.

Pedestrian and tourist-oriented amenities were part of the improvements to Jackson Square, the French Market, and the riverfront. After about a hundred years, visual and physical access to the Mississippi River and its activities were again possible in the heart of the city, restoring this powerful experience to both residents and tourists.

In 1984, New Orleans hosted another world's fair. The Louisiana World's Exposition, celebrating the city's relationship to water, opened to mixed national reviews, and like its predecessor in 1884, was a financial failure. Yet, among local and regional visitors, it was an unqualified success. Led by post-modernist Charles Moore, the fair's designers created festive public spaces enlivened with plantings of native trees, rapid-growing vines (such as kudzu, cat's claw, and morning glory), and one new introduction, mandevilla, now commonly seen in local gardens. More importantly, the fair left an urban legacy in the city's rediscovery of what had been industrial and warehouse spaces adjacent to the city's center. Today this neighborhood, now called the Warehouse Arts District, contains numerous art galleries and institutions, boutique hotels and upscale restaurants, hundreds of apartments and condominiums, and the city's newest urban park. Just minutes from both downtown and the convention center, the Warehouse Arts District is the center of the city's active and expanding visual arts district.

By the twentieth century's end, the community had become more cognizant of environmental and garden-related issues. The "green" professions have matured: landscape architects, garden designers, horticulturists, and suppliers are active and visible throughout the community. Designers and growers experiment with new plants and planting combinations and inspire local gardeners to try new approaches, particularly with native plants.

In addition, the city's active public art program often commissions local artists to create works for parks and green spaces. The general public understands the value of open space, and municipal policy endorses its increase. Urban

parks and nearby wilderness areas allow easy access to the region's natural environment and promote new understandings of its importance. Ongoing archaeological and historical research uncovers new information about how early residents used exterior spaces. And current marketing approaches to tourism emphasize unique aspects of the community's cultural heritage, broadly defined to include the region's physical environment as well as local traditions in music, architecture, and cuisine.

When woven together with other aspects of local heritage, the threads of the city's garden traditions create a rich cultural tapestry. Knowledge of the past increases an understanding of the community's horticultural evolution and prepares the city for an interesting and lively future.

Gaetano Capone, a native of Italy, painted French Quarter courtyard scenes when he lived in New Orleans in 1918–1919. He was one of several artists who documented urban life in early-twentieth-century New Orleans, helping to raise awareness and increase appreciation of the city's historic architecture. (The Roger Ogden Museum of Southern Art, University of New Orleans)

Public Parks
and Open Spaces

ROM COLONIAL TIMES, PUBLIC OPEN SPACES IN NEW ORLEANS have been central to the community's life. As the city grew, these spaces increased in number and evolved in character. Just under their green surfaces are lessons about the cultural, racial, economic, social, and political intricacies that have characterized the city from its earliest days. ❊ Many factors have contributed to the present-day city's form. Subdivision of land, following French colonial patterns rather than American ones, resulted in long, narrow parcels and street patterns with little relationship to logic or the compass. As plantations became residential tracts, new streets often met old ones at strange angles, creating quirky spaces randomly scattered throughout the city. Deeded to the city because they would not sell, these fragments became unexpected punctuations of green space, sites for later additions of plantings, fish ponds, or sculpture. Plans for new neighborhoods sometimes included small parks or tree-lined avenues as attractions. Drainage canals, built next to major streets, facilitated more residential development; as they were covered or filled in, broad boulevards resulted, often planted with rows of trees and blooming plants. ❊ In the nineteenth century's last decade, interest grew for open spaces that served the entire community rather than individual neighborhoods. This corresponded with national trends led by landscape architect Frederick Law Olmsted and his contemporaries working in cities throughout America.

City Park has many examples of artwork from WPA days. Shown here are works in the Botanical Garden by Enrique Alferez, left, and his contemporary Rose Marie Huth, right.

Cities built large municipal parks and incorporated elements of the City Beautiful movement into the public realm. Local legacies of this national movement are City Park and Audubon Park, open spaces that are among the most beautiful in the region. Along all major streets, mature tree plantings—mainly live oaks, but sometimes palms and crape myrtles—give testament to the foresight of those earlier in the twentieth century who wanted to beautify public spaces.

The result of all these influences is an urban crazy-quilt. While some of the components may lack the coherence found in other American cities, the parks and public green spaces of New Orleans certainly exhibit enduring charm and character.

City Park

The City acquired part of what is now City Park in 1850 from the estate of philanthropist John McDonogh. With later additions, this park now comprises more than fifteen hundred acres and is one of the largest urban parks in the United States. City Park is known for its many cultural and recreational attractions: the New Orleans Museum of Art; the Botanical Garden; lagoons and open fields; an array of sports facilities; a miniature train; horse stables; and a children's area containing a restored carousel. Some of the city's most majestic live oaks grow here, along with other native plants that replicate the landscapes of nearby swamps.

The City Park Improvement Association was organized in the 1890s, repeating a pattern of single-site governance established earlier for local parks. Most structures in the park,

City Park has many examples of the artwork of Enrique Alferez (1901–1999) including this one dating from the WPA days, located in the Botanical Garden.

OPPOSITE

Demonstration gardens, educational facilities, and meeting rooms are now part of the New Orleans Botanical Garden in City Park, with expanded and enlarged greenhouses soon to follow. Educational programs supply local gardeners with information on new plants, gardening techniques, and design ideas. Annual spring and fall garden shows are held here too.

including the entrance gate, the museum's original building, the peristyle, and the band pavilion, date from the early twentieth century and reflect the Classical Revival styles popular during the City Beautiful movement then taking hold in the American cities. Later, the Works Progress Administration initiated major improvements—City Park was Louisiana's largest WPA project—that implemented a plan from the early 1930s by Bennett, Parsons, and Frost of Chicago. Many features, such as bridges, benches, light standards, fountains, fences, and sculptures, were the work of local artists and craftsmen.

Efforts continue to enhance City Park attractions. The Botanical Garden has grown from its modest origins to include new educational facilities, demonstration gardens, and sizable collections of palms and orchids. Enlarged greenhouses and a new conservatory, expanding on elements designed in the 1930s by architect Richard Koch and landscape architect William Wiedorn, have been designed to feature plant collections and ecosystems from throughout the world. Important for local gardeners, too, are the ongoing educational programs in all aspects of native plants, cultivation techniques, and other garden-oriented topics. A resource library for garden enthusiasts is growing as well. When fully realized, City Park's Botanical Garden will occupy a major role in the garden life of the community.

Audubon Park

A state agency bought property for what is now Audubon Park in 1871. Little work happened on this site until the World's Industrial and Cotton Centennial Exposition of 1884–1885, and after the fair closed, civic leaders decided to develop the site into a public park. In 1887, correspondence began with John Bogart, an engineer who had worked in Frederick Law Olmsted's office on New York's Central Park and Brooklyn's Prospect Park early in his career. In 1893, the park's governing board communicated with both Olmsted and Bogart about designing the park, and Olmsted replied that he would first have to visit the site. Due to ill health, however, he never came. Appropriations did not materialize, and nothing came of this effort. By early 1898,

AUDUBON PARK (BEFORE)
VIEW FROM POINT "C" SHOWING EXCESSIVE FLATNESS OF EXISTING SURFACE, ALSO DITCHES, FORMALITY OF ROWS OF TREES, AND CONSPICUOUSNESS OF NEIGHBORING BUILDINGS

AUDUBON PARK (AFTER)
VIEW FROM POINT "C" SHOWING THE LIFE AND INTEREST TO BE EXPECTED FROM IRREGULAR LAGOONS WITH RICH WATER SIDE VEGETATION–NEEDED DRIVES AND NEIGHBORING HOUSES BEING HIDDEN BY LOW SHRUBBERY AND GROUPS OF TREES

PRECEDING SPREAD

Audubon Park, opposite both Tulane and Loyola universities, features a major pedestrial entrance on St. Charles Avenue, planted with seasonal color.

ABOVE

In 1898, the Olmsted Brothers proposed improvements to what is now Audubon Park. The conspicuous "neighboring buildings" are Tulane University, across St. Charles Avenue from the park's entrance. The proposal's drawings are the work of Arthur A. Shurtleff (later Shurcliff), who was instrumental in creating Colonial Williamsburg in the 1930s and 1940s. (University of New Orleans, Special Collections)

OPPOSITE

The Gumbel Memorial Fountain, at Audubon Park's St. Charles Avenue entrance, dates from 1919.

the park board had received proposals from Warren Manning and the Olmsted Brothers Office (the successor to the elder Olmsted's practice), perhaps the country's most prominent landscape architectural firms. No record remains of Manning's plan, but the Olmsted Brothers' proposal from 1898 included before and after sketches that mirrored illustrative techniques used by English landscape designer Humphrey Repton in his famous "Red Book" series of the late eighteenth and early nineteenth centuries.

In 1898, the board signed a contract with the Olmsted Brothers to design the park. Supervising the design and construction was John Charles Olmsted. According to newspaper accounts, he suggested that the park should contain elements of the local environment such as bayous, native plants, and "the architecture of the early settlers of Louisiana." Basic design work was completed in the 1920s, though the Olmsted Office remained involved with Audubon Park until the 1940s. Features, added over time, included irregular artificial lagoons, Beaux Arts pavilions and smaller structures, an elaborate gate and fountain at the St. Charles Avenue entrance, open areas of grass, a golf course, a teahouse, a carousel, mass plantings of native trees, and a large circular path. Most remain today, their impact enhanced by the maturity of the park's trees.

Though animals had been exhibited off and on in Audubon Park since the 1884–1885 expo-sition, a zoo was added during WPA days. By the mid-1970s, it had deteriorated so badly that it was called an "animal slum" and elimination seemed imminent. But with the emergence of civic interest, public and private funds were raised, and the facility was completely redesigned and refurbished by local landscape architects into an award-winning and popular attraction.

Today the park's zoo, together with the Aquarium of the Americas and the Louisiana Nature Center, are under the direction of the Audubon Institute. The importance of these attractions and their impact on the community cannot be underestimated. Designers developed innovative concepts of zoo exhibitry and planting design that are now commonly seen throughout the country. For instance, the Louisiana Swamp exhibit, opened in the early 1980s, was one of the first in the country to include the cultural context of the region's people—including food, music, and general lifestyle—while featuring native plants and animals as well.

More so than anywhere else in the city, the zoo's exhibits have enabled local residents to see firsthand how new ideas in planting design might apply to domestic situations. Over time, exhibits have been redesigned and reinterpreted, new features added, and new open spaces created, including a spectacular riverfront park. Though small by many urban standards, Audubon Park and its zoo are major amenities for the community.

With a golf course, a running/walking/bicycling track, meandering lagoons, lawns, mature plantings of trees, and access to the Mississippi River, Audubon Park is one of the most heavily used parks in the city.

Jackson Square

Military engineer Adrien de Pauger laid out the Place d'Armes, now Jackson Square, in 1721 as part of the colony's original plan. Placed in front of the government buildings and the colony's church, it was the site for ceremonial gatherings. In the 1820s, parallel rows of sycamore trees were planted on the square's sides as early attempts at beautification.

The government buildings—the Cabildo and the Presbytere, now part of the Louisiana State Museum—remain from the late eighteenth century, but the present St. Louis Cathedral (1849–1851) is the third church on the site. Flanking both sides of these buildings are the Pontalba Apartments, thought to be the first apartment buildings in America. They were speculative real estate developments built by Creole businesswoman Baroness Micaela Almonaster Pontalba, and in an effort to make her venture more attractive, she financed circular walkways and elaborate plantings in the square in the 1850s. Later, she raised money for a second casting of Clark Mills's statue of General Andrew Jackson astride his horse, and she prevailed upon city leaders to rename the square in honor of his service during the Battle of New Orleans in the War of 1812.

This space is the heart of New Orleans. With the facades of the Cabildo, St. Louis Cathedral, and Presbytere on one side, the four-story red-brick townhouses with balconies and lacy ironwork on two sides, the Mississippi River with twentieth-century improvements along the levee, and the manicured plantings of trees and seasonal color, Jackson Square is among the most beautiful urban settings in the United States.

While traveling in the American South in the 1850s, Frederick Law Olmsted visited New Orleans on several occasions. Though he was a newspaper journalist and not yet a landscape architect, his observations of the southern environment were keen and perceptive. In *The Cotton Kingdom: A Traveler's Observations on Cotton and Slavery in the American Slave States* (1861), he observed that Jackson Square was "now a

LEFT
This view of Jackson Square, circa 1855, shows the space after its midcentury renovation and the installation of Clark Mills's famous statue of Andrew Jackson.
(The Historic New Orleans Collection, 1948.4)

OPPOSITE
Today, Jackson Square is the image most people associate with New Orleans. Bordered on two sides by the Pontalba Apartments, it is one of the most memorable urban spaces in America.

No. 657. Birds-Eye View, Jackson Sqr. & River.

OPPOSITE

By the end of the nineteenth century, river commerce had effectively closed off visual and physical access between Jackson Square and the Mississippi River, seen in this image (circa 1880–1900) by local photographer George F. Mugnier. The circular walkways ringed with trees date from an earlier, midcentury renovation; the wharves and river commerce would remain well into the twentieth century. (Louisiana State Museum)

Although Père Antoine's Garden, a quiet green space behind St. Louis Cathedral, is populated more by birds and neighborhood cats than human visitors, all can enjoy its serene beauty from adjacent alleys and nearby sidewalks.

public garden, bright with the orange and lemon trees, and roses, and myrtles, and laurels, and jessamines of the south of France."

Few elements remain in the square from the nineteenth century besides the statue of General Jackson: there are four small marble statues tucked away in the corners and a few large cast-iron planters. The square's walkways, dating from a mid-nineteenth-century makeover, are now paved with aggregate dating from the mid-twentieth century. Due to changing tastes, uses, and periodic freezes, the plantings have evolved from rows of sycamores, citrus, and grass to magnolias, bananas, chinaberry, crape myrtles, and annuals. Some hardy trees, now mature, remain from the mid-twentieth century. Recent attention to Jackson Square's plantings by a local garden club and volunteers keeps the popular tourist area well maintained with seasonal color.

Jackson Square's orientation to the Mississippi River was interrupted for about a hundred years when wharves built after the Civil War blocked both visual and physical access. As port activities moved elsewhere and the tourist industry expanded in the early 1970s, a promenade was installed along the riverfront, re-creating one that was often mentioned in early nineteenth-century accounts of the city. Extending in both directions along the levee, this pedestrian space connects upriver to the Aquarium of the Americans and Woldenberg Park.

Behind the cathedral is a small fenced green space known as Père Antoine's Garden. According to legend, eighteenth-century grandees settled questions of honor here. This secluded spot, named for Père Antoine de Sedella, a popular, early rector of the cathedral who served from 1795 to 1829, is actually a cemetery for past rectors, including Père Antoine himself. Its fragrant sweet olive and mature sycamores and magnolias, with their veils of ivy, form a dense canopy over the gated park and provide a haven for songbirds and neighborhood cats.

Many of the nearby buildings have associations with writers such as Truman Capote, William Faulkner, and Tennessee Williams, and local artists who lived or worked here. Some artists still hang their works on the fence here and around Jackson Square, a practice that started over sixty years ago.

Washington Square

If you follow the directions given by Tennessee Williams at the beginning of *A Streetcar Named Desire,* you will, like Blanche DuBois, find yourself near Washington Square. Below the French Quarter in nearby Faubourg Marigny, this square dates from the early nineteenth century, though no plan exists of its original design. Like nearby Jackson Square, it features an iron fence, walkways, and mature trees; unlike Jackson Square, it does not have a statue of its namesake or prominence as a tourist destination.

The current design dates from a general overhaul in the mid-1970s, with play equipment added later. Mature oaks shade the perimeter, and a large open space in the center is perfect for the annual neighborhood festivals that take place here. Facing Washington Square are small-scale nineteenth- and early twentieth-century structures on two sides, a 1970s high-rise on the third side, and Elysian Fields Boulevard on the fourth. Nearby are some of the city's most interesting music clubs and restaurants.

Washington Square and its plantings of stately oaks and grass provide a sense of the community's residential scale and suggest the leisurely pace of nineteenth-century life in New Orleans.

Lafayette Square

In 1788, Spanish engineer Carlos Trudeau laid out Lafayette Square on St. Charles Street in what is now the city's central business district. Americans settled this section of the city after the Louisiana Purchase, and it became the city's center of banking, legal, and commercial activities. The square acquired its name in 1825 in commemoration of a visit to New Orleans by General Lafayette, and its surroundings grew dramatically during the third and fourth decades of the nineteenth century.

According to mid-nineteenth-century views, Lafayette Square was a fenced grassy space with interior plantings of trees. Gallier Hall (1845–1853), one of the South's finest Greek Revival buildings, faces the square and, until the early 1950s, housed City Hall.

Though it lacks a likeness of its namesake, Lafayette Square contains three significant sculptures: Henry Clay (1860), Benjamin Franklin (1926), and John McDonogh (1898), an early philanthropist whose legacy endowed public education here and created what is now City Park. The park's present character and urban role are different from its function in earlier times when important religious, commercial, educational, residential, and civic buildings faced the square. The city's centers of banking, business, and politics have since moved elsewhere, and Gallier Hall, a site for official functions, is all that remains of the nineteenth-century city.

In the 1970s and 1980s, Lafayette Square was the site of outdoor arts festivals and regular noontime concerts of local musicians. Today, with few planned events, little visitor traffic, and few pedestrian amenities, the square is a quiet oasis of mature trees, grass, shrubbery, and ground cover, accommodating transients more than locals. Yet, it is perhaps the most pleasant and accessible outdoor space in downtown New Orleans. With upscale residential projects, art galleries, hotels, restaurants, and pedestrian traffic increasing in the nearby Warehouse Arts District, its urban role may likely change again.

An 1852 lithograph, by B. F. Smith Jr. and J. D. Hill, depicts Lafayette Square from the tower of adjacent St. Patrick's Church. At that time, the square was fenced and planted simply with trees and grass. (The Historic New Orleans Collection, 1954.3)

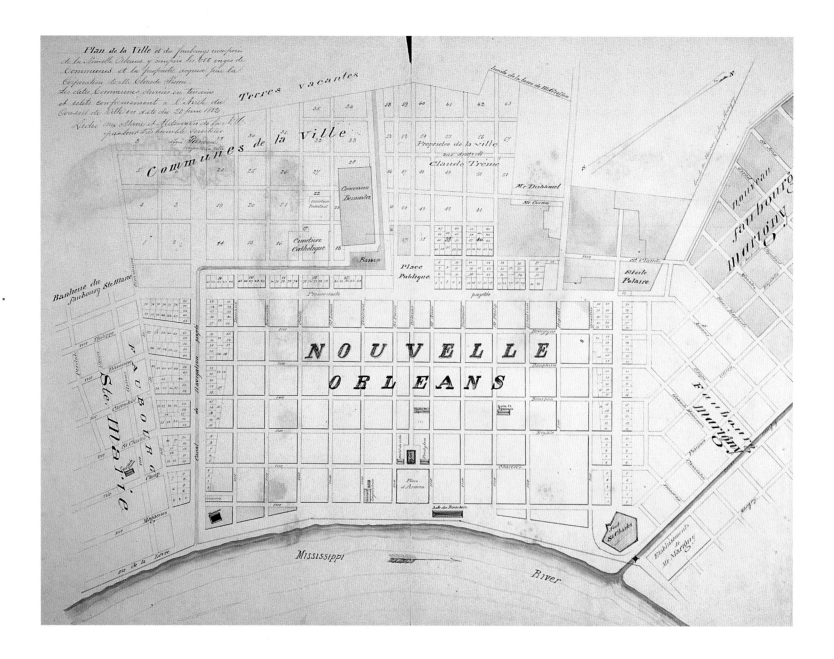

Congo Square AND Armstrong Park

For those particularly interested in African-American culture and the city's traditions of music and ceremony, no public space holds as much significance as the park now known as Congo Square. Located on the outskirts of the original city, this site has had a variety of names: Place des Nègres, La Place Publique, Place du Cirque, Circus Park, Circus Square, Congo Plains, Beauregard Square, and, finally, Congo Square. While its name has changed over time, its current and most enduring designation refers to its use in the early nineteenth century by the popular and celebrated Congo Circus.

Dating from early colonial times, this area was a public market and gathering place for African slaves and Native Americans. On Sundays, slaves and others of African descent congregated until sundown, dancing, drumming, singing, and selling food, vegetables, and other goods. Nineteenth-century writers described musical activities in Congo Square, and their accounts, some of the earliest of vernacular music in New Orleans, are primary sources for the study of jazz history. If any one place in New Orleans is ground zero for the birthplace of jazz, Congo Square is it.

The square, mostly a grassy area that accommodated commerce and public gatherings, was planted with sycamores in the early nineteenth century. Live oaks replaced the sycamores in the 1890s when the park's name was changed to honor Confederate General Pierre Gustave Toutant Beauregard, a French Quarter resident and local hero.

In the 1930s, the city built the Municipal Auditorium, which over time has held carnival balls, high school graduations, touring opera and circus productions, summer pops, jazz, and rock concerts, wrestling matches and ice hockey games, and even a temporary gambling casino. In another historical coincidence, Congo Square has retained its identity as a site for outdoor festivals and seasonal celebrations: the first Jazz and Heritage Festival was held here in 1969; Martin Luther King Jr. holiday activities are here; frequent music events are scheduled, and the annual canine parade of the Mystic Krewe of Barkus begins and ends here during carnival season.

In the 1960s the city demolished an architecturally and historically rich Creole neighborhood adjacent to Congo Square to build a cultural complex. The resulting space, inspired by Copenhagen's Tivoli Gardens, includes the auditorium, a theater for the performing arts, and the refurbished Congo Square. Opened in the mid-1970s, it was named for Louis Armstrong, a native of New Orleans. New plantings included shrubs and tropicals under the existing oak trees in Congo Square, sycamores along Rampart Street (grown from seeds taken on the first flight to the moon), and weeping willows along newly built lagoons. Other elements from this plan are paved plazas and grassy berms, a group of assembled historic buildings (one of which houses WWOZ radio station that broadcasts mostly local music), and a larger-than-life bronze statue of Armstrong by Elizabeth Catlett. There is also a ceremonial arch facing the French Quarter through which Mardi Gras floats passed on their way to carnival balls in the Municipal Auditorium (sadly, this doesn't happen anymore).

The park languished behind its intimidating fence, and the festive nature envisioned for the space never materialized. Over time, several development schemes were proposed, but for many reasons, none has taken root until recently. Now, the city and the U.S. Department of the Interior are planning to develop Congo Square and Armstrong Park into an urban national park devoted to the origins, development, and interpretation of jazz in New Orleans.

An 1812 map of the city after military ramparts and fortifications were removed indicates the location of Congo Square as Place Publique. Note the axial relationship to the Place d'Armes, now Jackson Square. (The Historic New Orleans Collection, 1966.33.30)

Annunciation Square AND Coliseum Square

The two largest open spaces in the mid-nineteenth-century city were Annunciation Square and Coliseum Square, located within blocks of each other in what is now known as the Lower Garden District. Shown in plans from the early 1800s as parks for the proposed residential neighborhoods, they have evolved in contrasting directions.

The Annunciation Square area did not develop as envisioned because of its proximity to the city's cotton press industries and river-front activities. Over time, the surrounding land remained industrial or underdeveloped; consequently, a cohesive residential neighborhood never evolved. The square originally had few features: its fence, like many others in the city, was melted to make Civil War munitions, and trees have been nonexistent for years. Municipal park improvements have been directed elsewhere in the city, and for the most part, Annunciation Square is unused. It may yet fulfill its early nineteenth-century promise if proposed new residential developments materialize nearby.

The Coliseum Square area, on the other hand, succeeded as a residential neighborhood from its beginning and remained viable until the late nineteenth century. Dormant and slowly declining for much of the twentieth century, it has survived various threats relatively intact and has been successfully reclaimed as a vibrant residential area.

The Lower Garden District is one of the city's most interesting areas because of its history, the inventory of surviving nineteenth-century structures, and the contemporary efforts to stabilize the neighborhood. Envisioned as the center of the city's intellectual and social life, Coliseum Square was the major feature in a grandiose, early nineteenth-century real estate development composed of classical Greek elements. Streets, for instance, bear the names of the nine muses of Greek mythology: Calliope, Clio, Erato, Thalia, Melpomene, Terpsichore, Euterpe, Polymnia, and Urania.

Coliseum Square's design reflects an early nineteenth-century solution to drainage: the Coliseum Street and Camp Street sides of the park were tree-lined canals that intersected and emptied into a semicircular basin at the lower end of the park. The Coliseum Street canal was filled in the 1840s and the Camp Street canal was covered by the end of the century. Although the city expanded rapidly during the 1830s and 1840s into this neighborhood, the area retained much of its rural feeling.

Houses originally occupied large parcels and often had lush ornamental gardens and fruit orchards. With growing pressures of urban expansion, these parcels were subdivided into smaller lots. One property near the square, advertised for sale in 1833, contained "improvements" consisting of "two spacious and well divided houses with galleries and their dependencies, two brick wells, two large cisterns, a well cultivated garden enclosed with hedges of orange trees and planted with a variety of fruit trees, shrubs and flower plants. There are, moreover, beautiful rows of orange trees, most of them bearing fruit, pecan trees, peach, plum, fig and plantain trees, two orange groves, several nurseries of sweet orange trees, a fish pond."

New residents were affluent, and soon, Coliseum Square houses were second in grandeur only to their counterparts in the nearby Garden District. Even during the closing years of the nineteenth century, Coliseum Square retained its pastoral setting of lawn and mature trees: an inventory in 1878 listed more than one hundred trees, including "China trees" (probably chinaberry), water oaks, tallow trees, and several unknown species. Additions to the square and its adjacent "finger parks" included circular plaster-over-brick basins for fountains and goldfish. Only one of three remains today, near the Race Street end.

By the late 1960s, many of the neighborhood's nineteenth-century structures had deteriorated into tenement houses. City and state authorities gave serious consideration to locating the second Mississippi River bridge here. The approaches would have destroyed the neighborhood much as the existing bridge corridor had unraveled the nineteenth-century fabric between the Lower Garden District and the central business district in the 1950s. Persistent efforts by neighborhood preservationists prevailed. Residents and property owners formed a neighborhood association in the early 1970s (it continues to be active today), and the neighborhood remained intact. Having stopped the proposed bridge and initiated widespread neighborhood renovation, this group secured city funding for the mid-1970s refurbishment of the park and pressured the state to remove an existing bridge ramp from a narrow green space along Camp Street. While much of the housing stock has been renovated, the neighborhood remains demographically diverse, and its residents are a quirky and lively group.

Like Washington Square downtown, Coliseum Square is residential in character and serves as a gathering place for the residents. The surrounding neighborhood, with its diversity of architecture, people, and commercial areas, is one of the most interesting places in town.

A view of Coliseum Square rendered by architect Thomas K. Wharton, who lived there from 1853 to 1862. In his journal on May 24, 1855, he describes his sketch: "The open square is carpeted with close smooth grass, and planted with luxuriant trees. It is more than one fourth mile long, and four or five hundred feet wide, surrounded with beautiful houses, and gardens filled with the choicest flowers, roses blooming all the year round, and at this particular season the air is almost oppressive with the luscious fragrance of the orange bloom and the different species of Jessamine, especially the 'Grand Duke' and 'Arabian.'" This picturesque scene is reminiscent more of an English village than one of America's major cities. (New York Public Library)

PLAN
DU JARDIN DU ROCHER DE STE HÉLÈNE

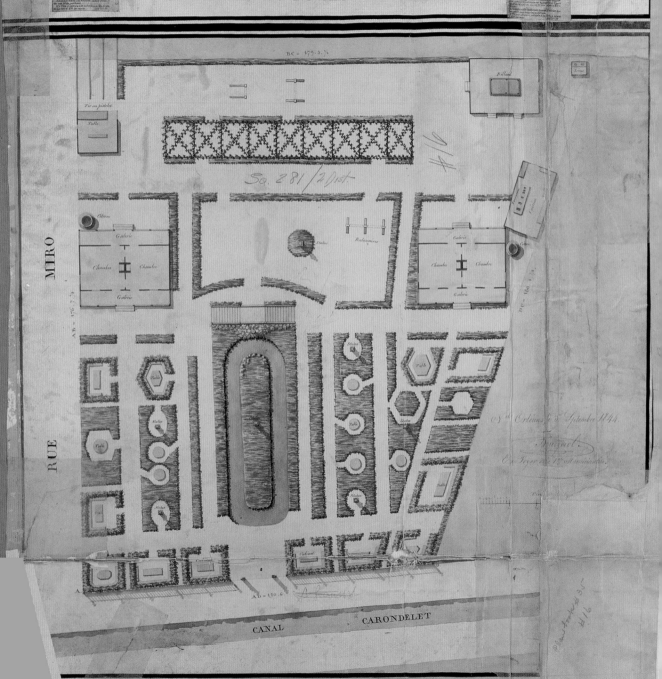

CANAL CARONDELET

A Nineteenth-Century Amusement Park

Other mid-nineteenth-century open spaces included private parks developed as public attractions. One such park, dating from its sale in 1844, was the Jardin de Rocher de St. Hélène. Its plan, one of the few extensively labeled gardens in the Notarial Archives, shows a definite design relationship to what was common in Paris in the first half of the nineteenth century. The garden was not large but included many features: walkways, grass panels with hedges, an island in an oval water basin, several statues, tables, and pavilions with galleries, an arbor, swings, a billiard room, cisterns, and a structure for cooking. While questions remain about who built it and what its purpose was, the plan gives a tantalizing view of a midcentury park in New Orleans developed for the public by private interests.

The Jardin de Rocher de St. Hélène was a privately developed amusement garden, dating from the 1840s. Among the various features are statues, an arbor, and a billiard room. (Plan Book 35, Folio 16; 1844; New Orleans Notarial Archives)

Linear Open Spaces

Being under sea level, New Orleans requires a complex system of drainage canals and pumping equipment to dispense runoff. Dating from the early nineteenth century to the present, these canals follow street patterns and give the city its unique pattern of wide streets and grand boulevards. Much of what appears to be a system of linear parks along many of the city's major streets, such as Napoleon Avenue, Elysian Fields Avenue, Louisiana Avenue, and parts of Orleans Avenue and Carrollton Avenue, are actually components of a complex underground drainage system. These and other linear "neutral grounds" have never been considered parks or connected to form an open space

system similar to Boston's Emerald Necklace; yet added together, they cover about three thousand acres, double the acreage in City Park. For the most part, the community enjoys these spaces in visual, rather than recreational, ways.

Other linear spaces popular with local residents include Bayou St. John, the Audubon Park batture, and the lakefront. Bayou St. John, with its late-eighteenth-century Carondelet Canal extension, was the connection between Lake Pontchartrain and the rear of the colonial settlement. Navigable until the 1940s and now dammed off at its upper and lower ends, the bayou sustains wildlife (turtles, ducks, herons, and the occasional pelican) and provides recreation for anglers and canoers.

The batture section of Audubon Park is one of the few places where visual access to the Mississippi River is possible. This is the upriver terminus for the popular tourist riverboats that connect the Aquarium of the Americas and Woldenberg Park, at the edge of the French Quarter, with the Audubon Zoo.

Lakeshore Drive and its adjacent green spaces accompanied post–World War II residential developments along the southern shore of Lake Pontchartrain. Nearby West End Park, at the city's northwestern boundary, dates from the late nineteenth century. As the terminus of a streetcar line, it was a popular park with amusements and restaurants. Almost five miles long, Lakeshore Drive has wide linear open areas that border two public universities and are popular year-round for evening and weekend recreation activities.

*W*est End was a popular recreation area for late nineteenth- and early twentieth-century New Orleans residents. Since the nineteenth century, this area on the western boundary of the city at Lake Pontchartrain has included the Southern Yacht Club (dating from 1849), West End Park, notorious nightclubs and beer halls, and popular seafood restaurants. This view, from around 1880, shows one of the restaurant pavilions in the Spanish Fort area of West End. (Louisiana State Museum)

OPPOSITE

The batture section of Audubon Park is one of the few places with visual access at ground level to the Missis- sippi River. Visitors can depart here for a leisurely downriver excursion to the Aquarium of the Americas, Woldenberg Park, and the French Quarter.

RIGHT AND
FOLLOWING SPREAD

Bayou St. John was an early Indian portage between Lake Pontchartrain and the Mississippi River. Used for maritime traffic until the 1940s, the bayou is now a serene linear reflecting pool for adjacent neighbor- hood residences.

Community Gardens
and Marketplaces

The city's latest horticultural overlay comes from recent Southeast Asian immigrants whose marketplaces have introduced Asian vegetables and fruits into the community. Their garden spaces, largely unknown to local residents, are reminders of how the community's horticultural traditions have grown and expanded over time through contributions from many different cultural communities.

Neighborhood gardens have sprouted in recent years as grassroots environmental groups spread throughout the city and immigrants sought to replicate gardens from their homelands. More than one hundred community gardens, projects of neighborhood associations or motivated residents, give a sense of pride and environmental awareness to older neighborhoods. New "green markets" bring farm-fresh produce to urban dwellers in the Warehouse Arts District and Uptown neighborhoods. And in eastern New Orleans, bustling farmers' markets provide the Southeast Asian community with vegetables and fruits from their homelands.

Unbeknownst to some, the gardens that nurture this exotic produce are tended by entrepreneurial immigrant farmers on undeveloped marshy property. These small, compact spaces are organized for maximum production of the ingredients common in Southeast Asian cuisines. Strolling through the early-morning market where the produce is sold is like visiting another country: English is not spoken, and non-Asians are definitely the foreigners. As this latest immigrant group is gradually assimilated into the local culture, the importance of their markets is dwindling; yet their horticultural contributions are becoming part of the city's multicultural cuisine and garden vocabulary.

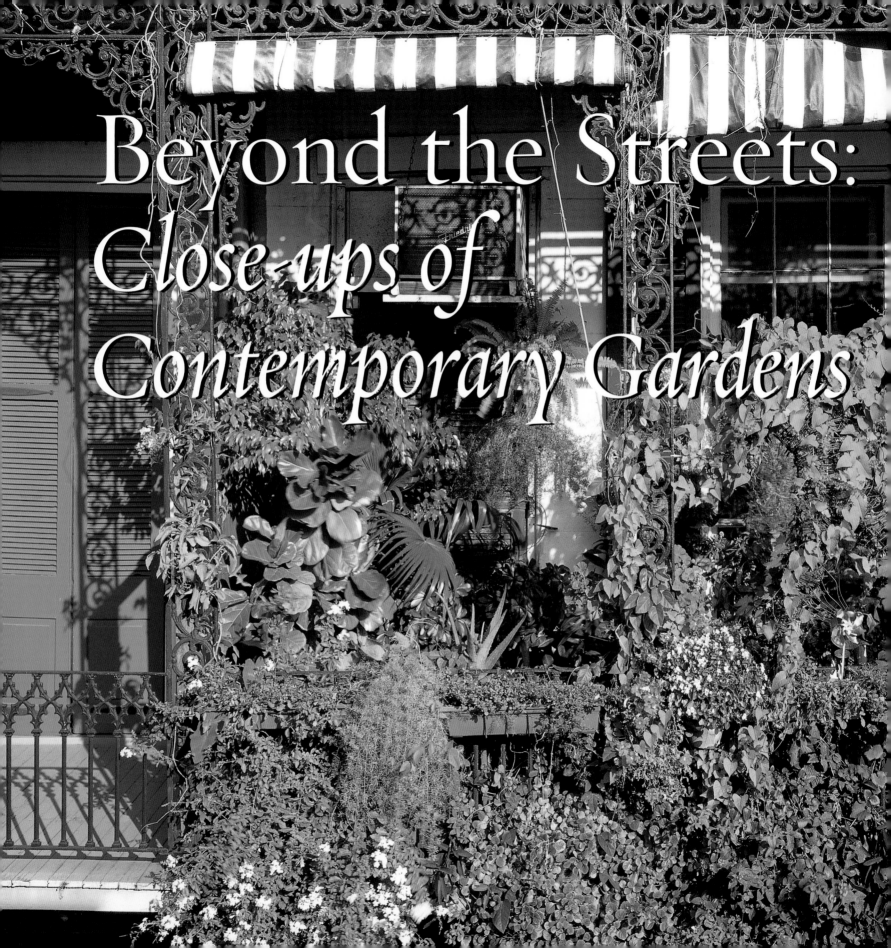

Beyond the Streets: Close-ups of Contemporary Gardens

PRECEDING SPREAD

Tricks of the trade

Caring for a balcony garden in the harsh New Orleans climate calls for inventive measures. Bill Huls uses a drop awning to fend off winter freezes, and a garden hose runs from the kitchen sink to combat summer droughts.

OPPOSITE

Quiet hideaway in a courtyard corner

White-flowering azaleas along a brick wall share space with fragrant night blooming jessamine and a sweet olive in Betty DeCell's courtyard on Bourbon Street. Adding more texture are pots of plumeria and clumps of ferns, gingers, elephant's ears, and Louisiana iris.

T HE PUBLIC SIDE OF NEW ORLEANS GARDENS, PLAYED OUT in the stitchery of parks, neutral grounds, and waterfront walkways, is there for everyone to enjoy. The private side, carved into the land around individual homes, is much harder to know. It's not that the gardeners aren't welcoming, for they usually are. But in the geographical sprawl of a city that has retained much of its low-scale, compact, residential character, there are far more gardens than even the most dedicated garden explorer could ever visit. ❋ Still, there are generalities that can be applied to the most prominent garden styles. Streetside balconies and galleries reveal much of themselves to any passerby who happens to look up, making them the most visible of private gardens. Courtyards, on the other hand, tend to be cut off from public view—except for fragments that can be taken in through a fancy iron grate or other piercing in a garden wall. Gardens created around a shotgun, cottage, or bungalow are somewhere in between. Their front- and side-yards line the streets of the city, but most have backyard gardens that are off-limits to strangers. Grand gardens are part public and part private too, but bigger and more formal than their more modest neighbors. Gardens filled with art tend to defy the rules—except the one that would limit the boundaries of the owner's imagination. House museums are open to everyone, providing knowledge of the gardening conventions of the past for the price of a ticket. ❋ To streamline the journey through the brimming storehouse of the gardens that sets the city apart from many of its urban cousins, sit back, take in the gardens of New Orleans, and enjoy the scenery.

Balconies, Galleries, and Porches

One of the best ways to savor the French Quarter is to pick a street bejeweled with architectural finery—Royal Street, say, or Dumaine. Stand at one end and simply take in the view. From this historic heart of New Orleans you can comprehend the beauty of graceful nineteenth-century buildings, especially the Mediterranean-inspired balconies and galleries, with their lacy ironwork and ornamental gardens.

The view from the downtown end of Royal, for instance, captures an aerial patchwork of plants, trailing above the street like dreamy fragments from a hanging garden of antiquity. It is one of Louisiana's great man-made vistas. It is just as lovely on a foggy, fall morning, brushed with sparkling dew, as it is on a winter evening, doused in sunset gold, or on a midsummer's night, drenched in the silvery light of a full moon. It is even wonderful on a sweaty summer day with the sky glazed a grim, gunmetal gray.

From the street, it is fun to imagine the aesthetics of gardening in the air, between the privacy of home and the bustle of the street. The concerns of balcony gardeners are not the same as those of their counterparts on terra firma. As a start, they must haul heavy pots, bags of soil, hoses, and the like up steep flights of stairs, through the living space, and out a window or door to the balcony. As with all container gardeners, they must water and fertilize most of the year. If a freeze is predicted, the plants must be covered or carried inside.

Besides the joy of working with subtropical plants such as hidden lilies, orchids, fan palms, and red passionflowers, amid the fragrances of gingers, angel's trumpet, and jasmines, the balcony gardener has an oasis for morning coffee, evening meals, and entertaining friends.

As an extra benefit, there's the front-row center perspective of the balconies and galleries that the pedestrian never sees. One gardener on a second-story gallery might look across the street to another balcony garden, or next door to another, and another, and so on, making the city's sense of urbanity more akin to Madrid or Paris or Havana than to Atlanta, Houston, or Chicago. Adding to that notion are the balconies and galleries that the pedestrian never sees—private ones overlooking courtyards and carriageways.

When New Orleans expanded across Canal Street and into the Garden District before the Civil War, the exteriors of the Classic Revival homes incorporated balconies and galleries as decorations. The architects knew it was wise to value the overhangs that shaded the interiors and allowed for open windows even during the rainstorms that pelt New Orleans through five-month-long summers. Balconies were built onto the sides of the houses, but they were more for style than for planting since there was no shortage of garden space around the sumptuous mansions in the elite neighborhood.

Much of the rest of the city takes its cues from the French Quarter, and many a plain-Jane post–World War II house has a second-story porch that is gardened in the tradition of Royal Street.

Gardens in the sky
The ambitious aerial gardens of Royal Street, seen against the backdrop of the business district, build on one another for block after block, creating one of Louisiana's great man-made vistas.

One balcony to another
An added treat for French Quarter gardeners like Chartres Street resident Lucy Burnett is the opportunity to get a right-on look at neighboring balconies across the street or down the block.

OPPOSITE
From galleries to porches
The idea of well-conceived sheltered space is a common thread throughout the neighborhoods of New Orleans. One example is the generous porch added to Barbara and Wayne Amedée's cottage near Audubon Park. Furnished handsomely and outfitted with convenient drop awnings, the porch provides a sumptuous view of a garden bursting with tropicals, natives, perennials, and flowering evergreens.

Bill Huls and Harry Worrell
THE FRENCH QUARTER

At first glance, the flora around the three-story townhouse on Royal Street in the French Quarter looks completely wild, as if it hadn't been touched by a pair of clippers since the terrible winter of 1989 froze the city to the ground.

ABOVE AND OPPOSITE
Blended balconies on Royal Street
Huls created an outrageous outdoor garden, lacing together a racy collection of vining plants. It got even better when another gardener moved in upstairs.

The growth is so thick that twining vines conceal the face of one entire side of the building and part of an upper-story window. The pair of balconies along the front offer a sight that is stranger still: long tendrils of exotic plants twine together and dangle so far down that they nearly brush the curbstones of Royal Street.

Even among the rarefied gardens of the French Quarter, the one that fluffs out from these balconies is a tour de force. Without the slightest nod to order, it sends a tangle of bleeding heart, passionflower, air-potato vine, and rosa de montana over the balcony railings like quilts hung out to dry. Snippets of flamboyant flowering plants pop out like starbursts. And

for comic relief, life-sized wire figures bound in twinkling lights appear to be climbing up the balcony railings.

Bill Huls, a landscape designer who lives in the second-floor apartment, has been tending his balcony garden for a decade or so. The garden had always drawn admiring comments from tourists passing below. But it wasn't until Neal Luke and Harry Worrell moved into the apartment above Huls's a couple of years ago that the two-tiered garden began taking on the mantle of brilliance. It was then that Worrell's air-potato vine, with its big, heart-shaped leaves, grew downward toward Huls's balcony, latching on to some rosa de montana which, in turn, began climbing upward. The quilt started taking shape.

Behind this profusion of plants, Huls often sits, taking in the feathery pink blossoms on the mimosa tree across the street and listening to inventive buggy drivers giving their tourist raps. Part of their repertoire centers around the Cornstalk Hotel across Royal Street and the cast-iron fence that gave it its name. "You can sit out here for thirty minutes and hear fifteen different stories about the history of the fence," said Huls.

When Huls isn't whiling away time on his balcony, he's working on it, especially in summer when the brutal afternoon sun beams down on the hundreds of container plants he has tucked into corners and along the railing. Huls used to spend hours every day filling a bucket in the kitchen sink and carrying it back and forth until everything was watered. He cut the time to forty-five minutes after he had the idea to rig a hose to the kitchen faucet and thread it through the bedroom and double parlors to the balcony. At one point, the hose goes over the molding on a door frame, a technique that keeps Huls and his friends from tripping over it.

Luke and Worrell live up a winding flight of stairs from Huls's apartment. Both retail display designers, they use the air-potato vine as the stylish mainstay of their balcony garden. Started from cuttings offered by a neighbor in the attic apartment, the vine comes back each year with no prompting whatsoever. Luke especially loves it because it reminds him of his great-aunt's home in the town of Chauvin, Louisiana, where it draped a side porch in cooling shade.

Like their neighbor downstairs, Luke and Worrell hang out on the balcony and have furnished it with comfortable tables and chairs. Awnings roll down to control the light and to create an instant shelter for the plants when freezes threaten. Doing double duty, too, is an antique chest of drawers used to store garden tools and serve alfresco meals.

"The view's great from here," said Worrell, stepping out on the balcony to take in the sea of slate rooftops and dormer windows spread out before him. "There's a breeze pretty much all the time, making it nice for gardening." He is quick to say that he doesn't know nearly as much about gardening as Huls does, but as he learns and experiments, the garden they are creating together is getting better all the time.

George Dureau
THE FRENCH QUARTER

Artist George Dureau has a gallery that wraps all the way around his cavernous apartment on Dauphine Street for 120 feet, like a deck around an ocean liner. He lives with the big double-hung windows to the balcony open until the temperature swings above what's tolerable. He is a die-hard New Orleanian, and for him that means toughing out the heat.

It helps that the gallery, covered with a sloping roof, funnels breezes and deters all but the most tumultuous, hurricane-force rain. It helps, too, that Dureau's gallery is so commodious that it can accommodate a forest of trees and plants that turn his home into a wild place where birds and a pair of squirrels he has named Georgette and Georgene drop in to visit. To add to the expanse of green, a neighborly bookseller once planted Chinese elm and sycamore trees in Cabrini Playground across the way. Then Christopher Friedrichs, a tree-loving landscape architect, came along and added sweet bay, along with white-flowering crape myrtles called Natchez. Forming a charming neighborhood forest, the trees buffer the sun and enhance Dureau's view of the pastel townhouses on one side and the gardens and basketball courts of a playground on the other.

Dureau—a celebrated painter and photographer, a theatrical storyteller, and a talented cook—is not a compulsive gardener by anyone's standards. If he is occupied with his art and the summer gets too hot or the winter too cold, he might let his plants fry or freeze, leaving the gallery awash in a brown sea of dead ficus, azaleas, rosemary, bromeliads, and ferns. That's where his gardening friend Mercedes White-cloud comes in, dropping by in her pickup truck with plants left over from nursery expeditions for her own French Quarter garden.

When the gallery looks decent, Dureau is likely to invite friends up for dinner parties. He sets out a dining table and piles it with napkins and stacks of blue-and-white dinner plates and maybe some potted sword ferns. Then he sets up a bar, lots of chairs, and little tables. And finally he cooks up some roasted chickens and a big salad and watches with his guests as night falls.

" 'Oh George,' a friend told me one night, 'this is like the best suburb of Paris!' " said Dureau, his brown eyes gleaming at the thought of it. "It was just a little rustic dinner, like at a country house. My dishes—well, no two match and I brought out all my mixed pottery and some of my French silver and all sorts of things."

His bohemian entertainments on the gallery sometimes get rather grand, as on the Sunday before Mardi Gras—Dimanche Gras, he calls it—when he lays out a generous buffet and arranges the plants into leafy bowers.

But most of the time, it's just Dureau, alone on his balcony, drinking coffee in the morning before he approaches his camera or his easel and starts the day. He tries to position himself discreetly so he won't be seen from the street, but it doesn't always work. "People pass by like they know me. They'll roll down their window and just call up and yell, 'Hello, George!' "

Above it all
Dureau often starts his day with coffee on the side of the balcony facing Cabrini Playground, then resets the table and invites friends over for a lunch of salad, spicy boiled crabs, and wine.

Entertainment garden on a wrap-around gallery
Dureau creates intimate spaces along a 120-foot-long gallery arranged with potted plants such as sword ferns, agaves, and palms.

White-blooming crape myrtles and other trees planted along the sidewalk transform the gallery into an urban tree-house.

Framed in
ornate ironwork
*Elegant cast-iron railings
and columns enclose
Dureau's home in
nineteenth-century grace.*

Nancy Monroe and Jim Amoss
FAUBOURG ST. JOHN

When architect Nancy Monroe decided to add a screened porch onto her family's roomy center-hall cottage in Faubourg St. John, she wanted it to function as a sitting and dining room that would flow out from the kitchen onto the spacious side yard. Taking in the view of two historically important streets, the porch would be cushioned by a large garden that combined vestiges of its former incarnation with additions made by Monroe and her husband, Jim Amoss. The streets especially intrigued Monroe. One of them, Esplanade Avenue, begins at the river and ends at City Park; the other, Bell Street, was once a portage for Native Americans encamped along Bayou St. John. Both thoroughfares bustle with cars and bikes and buses, as well as dog walkers and joggers moving through the neighborhood.

Monroe liked the idea of having a sheltering porch tucked into the midst of all this activity, where her family and friends could quietly dine, enjoy the garden, and witness the bombastic weather of New Orleans and the drama of the setting sun. The porch played into their notion that the 1910 house they bought in the 1980s could be adapted over the years to suit their needs. They had already converted the attic into bedrooms for their two children. Next came the porch, to be followed by an updated kitchen and, sometime in the future, a swimming pool.

The porch was designed to look as though it had always been part of the house, itself a hybrid of Arts and Crafts and turn-of-the-

century New Orleans architecture. So characteristic elements of the house were borrowed to compose the porch. The porch pilasters, for instance, echo the ones at the front entrance;

beaded boards along the edge of the ceiling refer to the undersides of the eaves around the house; and the measurements of the porch follow the proportions of the dining room, Monroe's favorite room. Screening was installed to look as if it had been an afterthought, tacked up one might guess, during a summer of bad mosquitoes.

Old feeling in a new screened porch
Monroe used tried-and-true architectural flourishes and the bright colors of the Caribbean to connect her family's 1910 house with its sprawling side-yard garden.

OPPOSITE
Room with a borrowed view
Beyond architect Nancy Monroe's freshly planted date palm and Arts and Crafts garage, the imposing presence of the house next door is a reminder that the garden is part of a tightly knit city.

To reinforce the city's tropical underpinnings, in both plants and architecture, Monroe
used X-patterned spindles for the railings and
a metal roof that would capture the random
rhythms of falling rain. The plank floor inside
is colored a deep sapphire blue and the ceilings
are painted turquoise and chartreuse, colors that
give the room a spicy glow.

When it came to the furnishings, Monroe
wanted them to be soft and comfortable and
able to accommodate large gatherings. "I wanted
furniture that had cushions, but I didn't want
anything so good that if it got rained on we'd be
horrified," said Monroe, whose design credits
include the Meridien Hotel on Canal Street and

collaboration on the stylish interior of Faulkner
House Books in the French Quarter.

With a cozy daybed, a chaise and an ottoman,
and a dining table and chairs, the porch does all
that Monroe hoped for. Little luxuries include a
fluffy potted palm and plants that come and go,
like a pink-flowering mandevilla or a spike from
a red-flowering banana. To shield the harsh
morning light, a white linen curtain can be
drawn. Hooks on the ceiling allow a chandelier
outfitted with candles to be moved as needed.

With the porch and its amenities, Monroe
found a way of savoring old customs for living
in New Orleans, even if they had to be fashioned from scratch.

Stephen Scalia and Milton Melton
THE FRENCH QUARTER

Balconies can hover above a busy public street or a sleepy private courtyard. Stephen Scalia and Milton Melton, the owners of a handsome 1820s Creole townhouse not far from the Mississippi River in the French Quarter, have both kinds.

One balcony, narrow and sparsely furnished, offers profoundly urban scenes over tree-lined Gov. Nicholls Street. Fragments of the bustling French Market can be glimpsed on the right, prettily planted neighboring balconies on the left, and, below, streams of chatty walkers and honking drivers come and go around the clock.

Three other balconies, the private kind, tucked behind the townhouse and a long brick wall, overlook the interior courtyard. Generous in spirit and size, the courtyard is a place where Scalia, a dedicated gardener, is apt to greet a visitor at the gate, hands smudged with dirt, pruners stuck in a back pocket. If the visitor is a gardener, he is just as apt to offer a baby staghorn fern or a pot of walking iris or a little crinum bulblet.

Over the forty or so years he has lived in this grand compound built in 1828 by a sister-in-law of Henry Clay, Scalia has created a work of art made up of formal and informal garden rooms threaded by thousands of plants. From sturdy natives to tender tropicals, the garden has a complex array of composed vignettes.

The gallery at the rear of the townhouse is especially groomed for sitting, drinking a cup of coffee or a cocktail, and enjoying the view. Merely ascending to the gallery on a wooden staircase shaded by a lofty white-blooming

OPPOSITE
Around a quiet fountain
Shade lovers such as staghorn and maidenhair ferns, palms, aspidistra, and ivy surround a fountain tucked into a brick wall.

Gazing up from a brick-paved garden
An outdoor room at the rear of the secluded compound owned by Stephen Scalia and Milton Melton points toward a spring-blooming redbud and the leaf-fringed facades of a slave quarter and townhouse built in 1828 by a sister-in-law of Henry Clay.

creamy white flowers atop soft new leaves like gifts to the Queen of the May. In summer, breezes play over the butterfly gingers, sweet olives, and crinums, blowing perfume through the French doors of the house. In fall, migrating birds pass through, stocking up on berries. In winter, plump grapefruits and kumquats and blooms of hibiscus and camellia and geraniums dangle from their branches like ornaments.

Down in a corner of the courtyard, a walled dining patio lies behind a cross-hatching of ferns, irises, and aspidistra, and a smartly pollarded sycamore tree. A lean swimming pool set off in boxwood, sweet olive, and potted shrubs makes a pretty picture across the way, followed by a velvety lawn of deep green grasses. Arranged into the shadowy crevices of stairways and loggias, timeworn pots and urns add layers of time and texture.

When Scalia and Melton bought the property from a Royal Street antiques dealer in 1960, the swimming pool, the dining patio, and even the beginnings of the crisscrossed pyracantha were in place. A game gardener, Scalia became an experimenter who has gained a lot of knowledge over time. He has learned about the plants of Louisiana and beyond, and how they will grow in a walled French Quarter garden.

"It's funny to think of it, but we've lived here longer than anyone else," said Scalia, stopping for a moment in his small library in the slave quarter. For most of its history, he said, the balconies overlooked livestock and laundry and worked as covered corridors to thwart the sun and the rain.

On the library walls, vintage photographs and prints show the garden over time. A

Ascending a stairway Crotons, hibiscus, white-flowering oleander, and espaliered pyracantha frame the stairway to the gallery at the rear of the townhouse.

oleander is a treat. What follows is the fun of settling into a comfortable chair behind a sumptuous screen of pyracantha trained to crisscross like a latticework fence. Better still is a visit on a winter's day when mockingbirds come to feast on the bright orange berries.

As you look out from this charming catbird seat, the beauty of the garden unfolds in a spiral of green that begins at the top of a fifty-foot-high southern magnolia and floats down through smaller trees and shrubs, and still smaller perennial and annuals, to the courtyard floor. In spring, the magnolia presents its

Natural tinkering
Tiny shade-loving plants make their own trails through gaps between bricks in Scalia's garden.

photograph taken in the 1930s by Frances Benjamin Johnston for the Works Progress Administration shows the slave quarter with laundry hanging in the foreground and a few pots of mother-in-law's tongue and geraniums. An earlier photograph of the same scene by New Orleans photographer Eugene Delcroix shows no plants at all.

Scalia doubts that there was ever much of a garden in the courtyard until the antiques dealer bought it and planted the magnolia, sycamore, and oleander.

"What we have made since then is not an English garden or a French garden," Scalia said. "It's just a very nice city garden with all the plants we like."

At the top of the stairs
Latticework painstakingly
made from a crosshatching
of pyracantha attracts legions
of hungry mockingbirds and
provides endless perspectives
of this sophisticated garden on
Gov. Nicholls Street.

COURTYARDS

French Quarter houses are shrouded in mystery. With their combinations of eighteenth- and nineteenth-century components gleaned from French, Spanish, and West Indian architecture, they are pedigreed exotics, poised to surprise and beguile.

Stare up from the sidewalk through a screen of shutters and you might see fragments of an ancient interior: a Venetian chandelier hanging from a ceiling rosette, a filmy mirror in a gilded frame, friezes of French wallpaper. Put your eye to a slot in a wooden gate and you may see a marble faun, a splashing fountain, maybe a white hibiscus tall as a tree. Gaze down the tunnel of an old carriageway, stuffed with potted bougainvillea and spiked yucca, and imagine a gardener who wants to recall the city's kinship with the Yucatan, across the Gulf of Mexico from New Orleans.

But to truly experience the charm of a house in the historic heart of New Orleans, it is necessary to enter the courtyard that lies hidden from casual sidewalk observation.

Only from the courtyard is it possible to survey the rich interior of a property—the house with all its idiosyncrasies, the garden walled by brick and sheltered by the sky. Over the years, the purpose of courtyards has changed: what were once simple passageways and service areas have evolved into thoughtfully designed gardens, and with the transition has come a time-honored landscape legacy found nowhere else in the United States.

Early gardeners brought all the bounty of a sultry tropical climate to their planting schemes, along with a sophisticated knowledge of European garden design. With their ideas, they created wondrous outdoor spaces with pavings of brick or stone, raised beds to escape a high water table, and pots and ornaments from the Old World. Around this general plan, they planted fruit trees such as fig, banana, kumquat, and satsuma for food and fragrance. Often a native magnolia was part of the scheme, along with gingers and jasmines and heat-loving bulbs such as crinums and amaryllis from around the world.

Eventually, these unique courtyard gardens became material for heady literary arias by writers such as George Washington Cable, Kate Chopin, Tennessee Williams, and Walker Percy. For sheer romance, it's always been hard to surpass the impressions of Lafcadio Hearn, a resident of New Orleans in the late 1800s. "A fountain murmured faintly near the entrance of the western piazza," he wrote of a courtyard he visited in 1879, "and there came from the shadows of the fig-tree the sweet and plaintive cooing of amourous doves. Without, cotton-floats might rumble, and street-cars vulgarly jingle their bells; but these were mere echoes of the harsh outer world which disturbed not the delicious quiet within."

Most New Orleanians and visitors to the city will never see privately tended courtyards such as these, but for the curious wayfarer who likes to ramble, there's the possibility of a solitary sojourn through the Quarter, peering through gates that give clues that a secret courtyard garden lies just beyond reach.

Perched over the landscape
At the rear of airy second-
floor parlors, a simple
balcony arranged for a
quiet evening grows dim
in the setting sun.

Mathilde and Prieur Leary
THE FRENCH QUARTER

Framing the view
The shadows of a tunneled carriageway give way to the light of a linear courtyard fringed with Chinese fan palms, Asian elephant's ear, bird-of-paradise, and sweet olive.

It's hard to beat the sensation that comes with entering the dark tunnel of a French Quarter carriageway and discovering the shadow-washed courtyard beyond. Gardener Mathilde Leary has slipped through this evocative domain of dark and light every day since she and her husband, Prieur, bought their porte-cochère townhouse on Dumaine Street in the mid-1990s. And still, she has not tired of ruminating on its special allure.

"When you're in the carriageway, you're on the outside looking in," said Leary, seated at the marble-topped table at the rear of her garden. "Then the sight of the courtyard sucks you in and suddenly you become part of the view."

It's a spatial adventure available only in the old part of the city—an adventure the Learys didn't have at their former home on a posh private street Uptown with big country-style gardens. There, they had room for a forest of trees that defined early twentieth-century sub-

urban style at its grandest. When they moved to the French Quarter, the setting changed in scope as well as feeling. Instead of a sprawling garden that surrounded their home like a garland, they had a small tailored one set into the walled interior of their property. Instead of a leafy greensward that summoned up the novels of Jane Austen, they had an urban *jardin* that recalled the photographs of Eugene Delcroix.

An inveterate traveler, Leary had long ago noticed how views are enhanced by a frame such as her carriageway. She noted how a French mountainside became something more when it was wrapped in the casement window of an alpine inn and how a slice of the Mediterranean took on added elegance when observed from a grape-entwined portico. But at the Leary home, nature doesn't make the view: the gardener does.

A gardener who predated Leary thought to put a fountain at the entry to the courtyard, creating a source of gentle sound that cushions the boisterous noise of the street. An orderly arrangement of old-fashioned plants gives the space classical form, and clipped sweet olives set against a two-story brick wall fill the courtyard with fragrance. Look up and there are waves of Lady Banksia roses and rosa de montana under-planted with pyracantha and sasanqua. Look down and there are beds of impatiens and ferns in moist raised beds set around a floor of mottled flagstone. And at the rear wall of the garden, a tiny woodland of crape myrtle and yew, roses

LEFT

Dining on the edge

Around a centerpiece of ivy, Mathilde Leary sets out salads and wine against a manicured bed of white and pink camellias, boxwood, and oleander, along with pentas, impatiens, nasturiums, and roses planted in pots.

BELOW

Sound of water

Parrot's feather nourishes a school of goldfish in a fountain edged with impatiens, holly fern, pyracantha, Asian elephant's ear, and mock orange.

and gingers form a backdrop for the table where Leary likes to spend time alone or serve meals to her family and friends.

She savors both the pleasures of her garden and the tribulations of growing the colorful plants she loves in a place defined by shade. She struggles with sun-loving pentas, bougainvillea, and oleander, coaxing them along and, when that's not enough, replacing them as needed— or expropriating sun-drenched spots on her street-side balcony.

She gardens with the eye of an interior designer solving problems in a handsome room cursed with a shortage of light. Roses are sent up walls where they can bask in the sun; ferns are kept low where they can hide in the shade.

Just as she uses flowers to add splashes of color, Leary uses her vast store of man-made props for the same purpose, as if the courtyard were a stage and she were a set designer. Among her favorite flourishes for a dinner party are candle-filled lanterns hung along the walls, brightly patterned tablecloths, napkins and crockery from Provence or Tuscany or Morocco arranged across the table, and exotic offerings of food and drink set out and ready to go. As her guests arrive at the carriageway, she treats them to the carefully assembled view, and within moments they are a part of it.

Betty DeCell

Just beyond the batten-board gate of a red, cream, and green Creole cottage on Bourbon Street, you're likely to find a blue bike parked against the alley wall. It's a sure sign that the landlady, Betty DeCell, is back in the courtyard going about her gardening. Continue along the fern-dusted alley and you'll run into DeCell, her hair wavy with humidity, her T-shirt smudged with mud. "Why, hello," she says in a whispery accent drawn from her childhood in North Carolina, guiding you back to the courtyard.

Accustomed to talking about plants and gardening with a passion that is as rock-solid as her accent, DeCell starts right in, describing her dreamy garden, beginning with the immense parasol of fruited banana trees fluttering overhead. "Things grow quite well here," she says, stepping into the exotic banana glade, "and the sound of rain hitting the leaves reminds me of being in a little tropical forest."

The courtyard is a near-perfect square bounded by the rear of the Creole cottage, two brick walls—one scalloped and dotted with pots of spiky agave—and the facade of a two-story outbuilding. Leading farther back into the property, an arched passageway arrives at a thick stand of arrow bamboo mixed with butterfly ginger, all set before a curtain of rambling clematis.

DeCell's courtyard, shared with her gardening tenant, writer Julia Reed, seems so old-fashioned that it could have been featured on a hand-tinted postcard of the 1930s. But in fact, it is forever being updated and changed as the gardeners, both inveterate experimenters, expand the horizon.

The garden today is much different from the way it was in the 1960s when Betty and her husband, Jack, first laid eyes on it. "Rosa de montana was growing thickly from the front house to the back house. It was the most romantic thing I ever saw," said DeCell, watching one of her treasured lizards scoot across a wall. "I never even went inside the house. I just said to Jack, this is it."

For one reason or another, many of the plants have disappeared over the years, including most of the rosa de montana that had tossed itself across the courtyard like an acrobat's net. But DeCell has never stopped encouraging the tropical ambiance she fell in love with on that first visit. She and Reed both love plants that smell good, so the garden is always steeping with the aroma of gingers or jasmines, plumerias and citrus, herbs, and more herbs.

Persistent management is everything in such a garden that seems so floppy and carefree. You have to know what to worry about and what to leave in peace. In the summer, hours go by as DeCell waters everything by hand, keeping an eye peeled for snails and other nettlesome critters. Lately, she's been adding a lot of newly available gingers to the garden, ordering them with abandon from a nursery in Morgan City, Louisiana.

She is quick to say that caring for her plants fills her days with purpose and happiness. It's a sensibility, she said, that goes back to her

Garden along the stairs
Crinum lilies, arrow bamboo, and potted duranta, agapanthus, and jasmine frame the stairs to the balcony of the rear building. Twining jasmine and rosa de montana trail around spider plants and rosemary on a brick wall.

Tropics in miniature
Fruited banana trees
thirty feet tall cover the
courtyard gardened by
Betty DeCell and her
tenant, Julia Reed. Wind-
tattered banana leaves
permit glimpses of the
brightly painted facade
of DeCell's nineteenth-
century Creole cottage.

Luis and Dianna Guevara
LOWER GARDEN DISTRICT

Landscape architect Luis Guevara would be the first to say that his patio garden is made from nothing more than bits of this and that. An assemblage of bits it may be, but each one is choice, and so is the garden.

Created from hundreds of plants with penetrating colors and textures, and an array of quirky containers and time-worn furnishings, the garden is as complex and full of meaning as a spice-filled Creole kitchen.

Guevara likes to call it his "recovery garden" because so much of what's there was on the brink of destruction when he brought it home to his patio on Euterpe Street, a rugged byway that leads to historic Coliseum Square in the Lower Garden District.

When a pair of battered cast-iron urns was banished from the garden of one of his landscape clients, Guevara lugged them home, knowing they would come in handy. When a teakwood Giverny bench had outlived its usefulness following the New Orleans Museum of Art's Monet exhibit, he hauled that home too. The same went for a batch of straggly black bamboo, some neglected angel wing begonias, all sorts of ferns, and a rangoon creeper.

The challenge was to take all these disparate elements and organize them into a stylish whole.

It doesn't hurt that the long and narrow patio is part of an exquisite 1850s Greek Revival townhouse that Guevara and his wife, Dianna, allow to show its age in a neighborhood that doesn't court anything pristine. Peeling paint abounds around Guevara's patio, surrounding

Long and narrow
On a bed of cracked concrete, landscape architect Luis Guevara established a garden of potted plants that range from workaday to rare. This view toward his dining room takes in compositions of white spiral ginger, black bamboo, walking iris, impatiens, and lady palm.

balconies are warped and disheveled, moss coats the brick, and cracked concrete paving and fallen leaves cause no alarm.

The mood is enhanced by the French Quarter technique of gardening in pots to ensure good drainage and the option of moving plants around on whim. All of this helps create a tropical ambiance where compulsive maintenance seems beside the point.

"I've always thought of this garden as looking run-down," said Guevara, a warm-hearted man who speaks with a hint of his Cuban homeland. "I call it my Tennessee Williams garden because it looks like a set in *Streetcar Named Desire*."

The garden's unifying force is Guevara, whose design credentials include work on Audubon Zoo, Woldenberg Park, the New Orleans Museum of Art, and, more recently, the luxurious Lakefront home of New Orleans chef Emeril Lagasse.

Even in this little unplanned garden, Guevara shows the skill that makes him one of the city's foremost landscape architects: unwavering grace and a thoroughgoing appreciation for Louisiana's native plants and the exotics that complement them so well.

Step out of a wide door that leads from the house to the garden and you immediately see how Guevara can transform random objects into arrangements as classic as knights' moves on a chessboard. One vignette features the discarded teakwood bench flanked by the rusty urns stuffed with walking iris. Billowing around and overhead stands a sheltering bower of chinaberry and American elm trees, flame azaleas and rhapis palms.

The morning sun filters through the opaque leaves of the trees, brushing all that is beneath with a soft, dappled light. Off to the rear, a sweet bay that the Guevaras use for cooking and a red banana that they plunder for cut flowers adds a layer of polish. To the left, there's a gigantic angel-wing begonia, its pink flowers arranged in thick, dangling balls. Along the narrow walk, borders five feet deep harbor layer upon layer of plants packed so densely that the pots holding them are practically invisible.

"I think of small gardens as jewels that you enrich with texture and interest," Guevara said of his patio. "In a garden like this, everything is significant."

Molly Reily
THE FRENCH QUARTER

When Molly Reily got hold of a Creole town-house on Royal Street in the mid-1990s, she got something that most French Quarter home buyers wouldn't want—a huge, concrete-paved parking lot where the courtyard should have been. Not at all put off by such a flagrant lack of charm, Reily relished the chance to make something fresh and offbeat, a break from the prototypical Quarter garden of big trees and big shade. Instead she was determined to create a sunny plaza where she could grow flowering, fragrant plants, especially her favorite, the rose.

Extensive restoration of the house and construction of a guesthouse in the rear meant following the proscribed rules of the Vieux Carré Commission, the French Quarter's preservation agency. But where the garden was concerned, Reily had free reign. She mapped out a no-nonsense, geometric design that would work as a garden as well as an outdoor room. The plan was composed of three side-by-side rectangles flanked by slim borders and a stepped entrance that clearly delineated the garden from the house. As she saw it, the rectangle in the middle would be a smooth swath of grass, the one on the right would be a swimming pool, and the one on the left would be a bed of flowering annuals and perennials.

Reily showed her sketches to her friend Betsy Smith, a landscape architect based in New York. Smith translated them into carefully scaled working drawings and, as a practical flourish, broke the flower bed into three parts to ease the job of the gardener. She suggested the types of plants she thought would look right in such a space. Then landscape designers John Parrott and Kim Alvarez came up with a selection of plants that would thrive in the New Orleans climate and, at the same time, suit the scale of the garden.

Sitting at the desk in her pleasant study on a summer morning, a bowl of musky old-garden roses placed nearby, Reily explained the evolution of the courtyard, a process that she thoroughly enjoyed. She produced a scrapbook of photographs of the grimy parking lot and its gradual transformation. A couple of pages were devoted to the excavation for the pool, a stage that Reily hoped would be accompanied by the discovery of a trove of nineteenth-century pottery and bottles. Although the hours spent sifting through the muck produced little more than broken pottery, china, and glass, it was one of a series of experiences that connected Reily to her new home.

The landscape designers moved in to lay out the rest of the courtyard, filling it with truckloads of rich soil and then plants and trees, many of them mature specimens that gave the garden the look of instant age.

Against the wall by the swimming pool, they planted Capitol pear trees, a slender

Greening of a parking lot
Mixed petunias and other brightly flowering annuals announce the steps to Molly Reily's sun-drenched courtyard, created in a space that for years was used for parking cars. The land was organized into three rectangles—a swath of grass in the middle, flanked by a cutting garden on one side and a swimming pool on the other.

allows, the gardening chores include diving into the pool with her pruning shears to keep the plumbago and pink indigo trimmed just above the waterline.

"Houses in the French Quarter are like farms with plots," said Reily, who grew up in Winston-Salem, North Carolina. "Everything is contained and private."

But Reily doesn't keep her courtyard for her private pleasure alone. She uses it often for entertaining, employing the kitchen in the guesthouse as a staging area. Each Mardi Gras morning, she invites more than a hundred friends and neighbors to a party that has become famous for its generous hospitality. If Carnival falls in late February, Reily's sweet olives and roses are blooming and buds are forming on the Confederate jasmine.

Enjoying the benefits of an enchanting garden with sweet-smelling plants is one of the great joys of life, Reily said. One of her favorite times to enjoy her garden comes in the dead of night when she can look out the windows of her second-story living quarters and watch the moon overhead, bathing her courtyard in its blue glow.

relative of the Bradford; *Camellia sasanqua* 'Sparking Burgundy'; bloodleaf bananas; Chinese fan palms; plumbago; and cleomes and pentas.

Along the opposite wall are Little Gem magnolias, along with hollies, hydrangeas, lilies, leatherleaf ferns, butterfly ginger, and mint. Standard roses accentuate the geometry of the garden; antique roses lend it warmth and fragrance.

Reily works there each morning after walking her poodles, Pete and Chou, through the French Quarter. When the weather

LEFT

Quiet and composed
Reily often entertains in her courtyard, using her guesthouse kitchen as a staging area. Along the edge of the pool, dreamy mosaics of bloodleaf banana, plumbago, philodendron, sasanqua, and pear trees give a feeling of privacy. Toward the rear, Chinese fan palms are mixed with simplicity rose, sweet olive, and banana shrub.

OPPOSITE

Spatial curiosities
A stately edge fashioned from trees and clipped parterres gets gratuitous structural clout from a two-story slave quarter next door. Reily's border is arranged with carefully trimmed Little Gem magnolias and evergreen hollies. Antique and modern roses, along with colorful perennials and fragrant herbs, fill the boxwood-enclosed parterres.

Henrietta Hudson

FAUBOURG MARIGNY

OPPOSITE

Framed by cypress and crape myrtle
From her petite porch, Henrietta Hudson can look through the twining floral mosaic she has created, out to the goings-on along the busy street.

BELOW

Layer upon layer of billowing green
Hudson's brilliantly layered garden, which changes dramatically from month to month, can be counted on to slow down traffic on Burgundy Street.

Set amid a block-long stretch of tame gardens in Faubourg Marigny, Henrietta Hudson's tiny landscape is a brilliant showstopper, awhirl with rare perennials, flowering trees, and ravenous vines that waft around the Victorian columns of her front porch like billowing sails around tapered masts.

When the wind is still, the garden is a tapestry of colorful blooms and myriad greens; when the weather acts up, the slow motion increases to fast-forward. Thick tendrils of rangoon creeper and thunbergia in shades of pink and ocher take flight, shaking the tall stalks of Formosa lilies and red pentas, which in turn rattle the oleander and the bougainvillea. All of this, in turn, shakes the hibiscus and turk's cap, the mahonia, and the ruellia, along with hundreds of other plants Hudson has acquired from friends, nurseries, and plant sales around town.

Off on the street side of Hudson's sidewalk, a white-blooming crape myrtle and a fluffy bald cypress arc over the porch—one a reminder of nineteenth-century New Orleans gardens, the other a reminder of the city's ancient swamplands. Come fall, the crape myrtle is the first to lose its leaves, followed by the cypress, which drops rust-colored winter foliage to the ground in mounds of ready-made mulch. Such shenanigans are always going on in Henrietta Hudson's Burgundy Street garden.

From the lone chair that furnishes her porch, beside a table just big enough for a book and a glass of iced tea, Hudson can pick out all the players as they arrive and depart with the seasons. Surrounded by her ever-present cadre of three cats and one dog, she is the producer of a grand show staged for one.

Sometimes people try to call Hudson's creation an English garden, but she will have none of that. "I just stuck stuff in the dirt, hoping for privacy and beautiful color," she said, her cropped hair pushed back, her lips brushed Chanel red. "When I moved here I thought, thank heaven, I finally have sun and dirt together."

Reared far upriver in Cairo, Illinois, Hudson lived more than half of her life in the French Quarter, where she gardened in the deep shade of a small patio and learned all she could about how plants grow in New Orleans. Most evenings, she abandoned her dim patio for the wooden stoop at her front door and visited with friends as they headed to a nearby grocery store. Hudson's stoop became a raucous gathering place—complete with wine and cheese and bonhomie—until she bought her house in Faubourg Marigny and moved a mile away.

At the new house, a two-bay shotgun built in the 1860s, the porch became her stoop and

more. None of the old friends were there, and
the people in the new neighborhood were not as
apt to visit, but she saw the porch as a backdrop
for other kinds of creatures—the kind with
wings and tails and paws and fur.

Because of the garden's density and the profusion of plants oozing with berries and nectar,
wildlife is on a nonstop parade. Butterflies and
dragonflies, bees and salamanders zip from one
plant to another, doing their dance of chase and
flee. Birds as unobtrusive as hummingbirds and
as bossy as blue jays twirl through the velvety
thickets, sometimes nesting there and training
their young.

Along the driveway beside the porch,
another garden adds yet another dimension,
beginning with a peach-colored angel's trumpet
that branches over Hudson's parked car and
flowers year-round unless there's a freeze. In
summer, blustery Disney ginger offers ongoing
tomato red blooms and around a bend stands a
greenhouse stuffed with garden tools, thousands
of bromeliads, and a Dutchmen's pipe vine that
fairly drips from the rafters.

That's the private part of Hudson's garden
that few ever see. For most, the vision of her
splendid porch and the floral hubbub around it
are more than enough to contemplate.

Geraldine and Willie Veal
THE NINTH WARD

Sitting on Geraldine and Willie Veal's deep porch on a hot summer morning is one of the quintessential New Orleans experiences. Tucked behind a broad white aluminum awning with green stripes, the porch offers deep shade for watching the comings and goings on Congress Street, a well-traveled route in the city's Ninth Ward, not far from the burly shipping channel known as the Industrial Canal.

The Veals live in a remodeled double shotgun painted white, with a backyard long ago given over to three strapping dogs, each of which has a wood-frame house of his own made by Willie Veal. With no backyard to till, Geraldine Veal makes up for the loss with a forest of old-garden and hybrid tea roses planted on every remaining patch of dirt along the sides and front of the house.

Veal has lived in this blue-collar neighborhood her entire life, and her gardening efforts lend charm to the gritty scene that mixes civility and blight side by side. She does it with towering rose bushes, fluffing out in great sprays at the top, nearly touching the roofline along each side of the house and sweeping around the front corners to shield the porch behind a fragrant privacy screen.

The garland of roses does exactly what Veal wants: it puts an ornate halo of her favorite flower around her trim, practical home, giving it just the right touch of old-fashioned friendliness.

Every morning around ten and every evening around sundown, she grabs her clippers and passes by her roses, inspecting each plant, nipping yellowed leaves, snapping tiny dried branches, and applying water as needed. Every winter she reminds her husband to get out his ladder and trim back the roses from the top, cutting them a foot or so lower than the window frames. She doesn't fertilize, recalling that the one time her husband insisted on trying some synthetic food, the roses died back.

Her guidelines for raising the roses are the same ones she has used for her children and her pets: consistency and a caring heart. "I'm very delicate with the roses," Veal explained, "and the roses are delicate with me."

The daughter of a flower-loving mother, Veal bought her first roses more than twenty years ago from a family-run nursery near City Park. She came home with a couple of pots of Mrs. Dudley Cross—full, pale-yellow roses tinged with pink and blessed with a robust

BELOW
Eye for symmetry
Old-garden roses, Mrs.
B. R. Cant, left, and
Mrs. Dudley Cross, right,
flank the shady porch of the
Veals' white-frame cottage
in the Ninth Ward.

OPPOSITE
View along
Congress Street
Roses that began as cuttings
and ornamentals that began
as potted Christmas gifts
make a hearty contribution
to the Veals' street.

constitution that keeps disease at bay. They were staked in the ground with broomsticks, without benefit of root stimulant or compost or fertilizer. They took off and grew right away.

Veal made cuttings and stuck them into the hard, scrubby ground. Soon she added more cuttings from a neighbor's luscious specimen of Mrs. B. R. Cant, a cabbagelike, prolifically blooming, pink tea rose treasured throughout New Orleans since the early 1900s. Over the years, Veal's children have brought her more roses and the collection has expanded accordingly. The Ninth Ward garden has become an attraction of sorts, beckoning local rosarians and out-of-town experts.

So far, the collection includes Cecile Brunner, a charming 1880s rose with fragrant pink blooms; Chrysler Imperial, a 1950s hybrid tea rose from Germany with big, deep velvety-red flowers and dark green leaves; assorted ramblers; and one that she will admit is her favorite—Mrs. Dudley Cross.

"This is a beautiful rose, just coming out," said Veal, stopping at her ten-foot-tall Mrs. Dudley Cross and snipping off a creamy bud just beginning to open. The bush was lush with roses in full bloom and buds ruffling around the edges. "I don't usually bring my roses inside," she went on, winking at a little girl coming along the sidewalk, "but my neighbors do."

As far as Geraldine Veal is concerned, these roses—along with intermittent sprinklings of holiday geraniums, lilies, and poinsettias—are plenty enough garden for her, and all the garden she has time for. Hers is the kind of landscape she was raised around, the kind she is offering to her neighbors, and the kind she is passing along to her children.

Louis Aubert
CARROLLTON

It's not unusual to find a tumbledown shed or even a chicken coop in the backyard of a New Orleans cottage or shotgun. Relics from the days when laundry was hand-washed and eggs were home-hatched, the buildings are fading reminders that rear yards were once utilitarian work spaces essential to running a household.

Most of the coops are gone (it's illegal to have more than a couple chickens in a yard these days), but a lot of the sheds have survived. Some are still used for washing clothes, others are used for storage, and still others have been recycled beyond recognition.

One shed that fits perfectly into the last category is tucked behind a small Arts and Crafts cottage on a quiet street called Neron Place, not far from Tulane University. Once a stark cube of concrete blocks housing a washing machine, a makeshift toilet, and a nook for gardening supplies, the shed has been transformed into a cheery garden folly by its owner, Louis Aubert. An interior designer and color specialist, Aubert has spiced up the paint on homes, hotels, and condos all over town.

First Aubert painted the shed a rich taupe to match his house. Next he outfitted it with a fanciful array of architectural details. Round cast-stone finials were affixed to the corners of the roof; Bermuda shutters lent symmetry to the facade; and blushing New Dawn roses were woven around a wooden pergola. Soon a fountain with nymphs frolicking on concrete scallop shells went in, along with a geometric backdrop

Making the best of a shed Louis Aubert transformed his shed, once a stark cube of concrete blocks, into a cheery garden folly with fake topiary made of fig vine, a wooden pergola laced with New Dawn roses, and Bermuda shutters.

red berries prized by migrating songbirds. Hidden in alcoves carved into the garden's dense foliage, lilies, crinums, plumbago, shrimp plants, and lush tropicals add another dimension.

Like the slow, thoughtful renovation of the house, guided by old-fashioned ways of keeping things airy and cool, the garden eventually took on the character of a mysterious old Louisiana landscape with a powerful history behind it. Its depth can be traced back to Alicia Heard's childhood on a working sugar plantation

outside of St. Martinville, a courtly, French-speaking town in Cajun Louisiana. There she learned to identify plants and to appreciate the art of landscaping. She meandered through the Jungle Gardens of naturalist Edmond McIlhenny at Avery Island as well as the garden of early American actor Joseph Jefferson on Jefferson Island. But her favorite garden was the one created by the eccentric artist and preservationist Weeks Hall at his home, Shadows-on-the-Teche, in New Iberia.

She was captivated by the quality of the light and the powerful native foliage that Hall wove through his garden, and the quiet and disquiet that it demanded. She was drawn to the strong, primeval plants he preferred—live oaks, Spanish moss, magnolias—and the way he combined them with old-fashioned, flowery ornamentals such as camellias, wisteria, and swamp crinum. She particularly admired the cloak of giant bamboo that surrounded the perimeter of his property like a palace guard.

When the Heards got their house on Louisa Street, Alica knew her plants and she knew her gardens. But she was not yet a gardener. "I learned the mechanics by trial and error," she said, sitting at the dining table drinking strong coffee, her dogs Pollo and Zelda at her side. "But I always knew what I wanted the garden to be like. I wanted it to feel immediate even though you were sitting in the house—the way that gardens were before air-conditioning came about."

Grand Gardens

Most of the grand gardens of New Orleans can be found by heading Uptown from the French Quarter, through miles of neighborhoods that lead to the old suburb of Carrollton. It's a trail covered by the St. Charles Avenue streetcar, a charming mode of exploration. As you peer out the streetcar windows, the homes along the avenue—with their ornate iron fences, oaks and magnolias, sprawling lawns, and gigantic shrubs—give the impression of an awesome linear park. Getting off at the Lower Garden District, the Garden District, the University Section, and Carrollton—contiguous landscapes geographically as well as chronologically—you can experience thousands of thought-provoking gardens on foot.

This is the terrain pioneered by wealthy Anglo-American families who were not at home with either the ingrained culture or the compressed space of the French Quarter. They built mansions on large lots, creating a spectacular model of late-nineteenth-century suburban life.

Much of the land had been occupied by plantations growing cash crops as well as fruits and vegetables for planters and their families. The Garden District, for instance, was built on land subdivided from the immense Livaudais plantation, and many of the new homes employed plantation gardening styles: old-fashioned plants, many of them fragrant, impressive shade trees, and classical grids.

*Gardens on
the streetcar line*
*Treasured streetcars follow
a route along St. Charles
Avenue, passing miles of
stately Uptown neighbor-
hoods that are home to many
of the city's grandest gardens.*

Taken as a whole, the Garden District is a composition of opulent houses joined together by rambling gardens featuring big trees, dark green foliage, and seasonal flowering shrubs and annuals. They are strong and established, rarely fragile or tentative. The style was refined over the years by twentieth-century designers who reinterpreted the garden sensibilities of earlier times. Contemporary designers and landscape architects such as René Fransen, Luis Guevara, Michael Carbine, Vaughn Banting, John Mayronne, John Parrott, and Melinda Taylor owe a lot to their predecessors, Richard Koch, William Wiedorn, Dorothy "Baby" Hardie, and Christopher Friedrichs.

Writer George Washington Cable, an observant gardener known to ramble often through the grand gardens of Uptown New Orleans, described firsthand the moody magic these landscapes can evoke in an essay called "The Mid-Winter Gardens of New Orleans," published in 1914:

One night—oh, oftener than that, but let us say one for the value of understatement—returning to our quarters some time before midnight, we stepped out upon the balcony to gaze across into that garden. The sky was clear, the neighborhood silent. A wind stirred, but the shrubberies stood motionless. The moon, nearly full, swung directly before us, pouring its gracious light through enormous cross-hatchings of the pecan, nestling it in the dense tops of the cedars and magnolias and sprinkling it to the ground among the lower growths and between their green-black shadows.

LEFT
Winter wonderland
Billowing Carolina jessamine
and fluffy azaleas in pink
and white turn an ordinary
sidewalk into a wondrous
path along Louisiana
Avenue—a lush boulevard
that forms one of the boundaries of the Garden District.

RIGHT
Tangles of iron and oak
Like hundreds of architecturally significant structures in
New Orleans, the Italianate
Revival facade of this mansion in the Garden District
lends a mighty backdrop to
a time-honored landscape.

Johann and Bethany Bultman
THE GARDEN DISTRICT

At first glance, the home of Johann and Bethany Bultman on Louisiana Avenue looks like a standard Greek Revival, plantation-style mansion with all the trimmings. There is a front gallery, for instance, and a center hall. Dormer windows poke out from the roof, and the exterior is white with green slatted shutters. A longer look, though, reveals a decidedly unconventional room hitched to the right side of the house. One and a half stories high, fitted with graceful windows and known as the Garden Room, it is filled to the brim with paintings, sculpture, high-style wicker furnishings, and ornate ironwork—all arranged under a gnarled forest of fiddleleaf ficus that stands nearly thirty feet tall.

Aside from its idiosyncratic character, the room is noteworthy for its place in the city's literary history.

It was used by Tennessee Williams as the inspiration for the set of his Southern gothic play, *Suddenly, Last Summer.* In the play, the room, with its strange tropical aura, is a metaphor for the relationship between Violet Venable and her son, Sebastian. In the production notes, Williams describes the room, which he came to know in the 1930s during a two-month stay with Bultman's grandparents: "The interior is blended with a fantastic garden which is more like a tropical jungle, or forest, in the prehistoric age of giant fern-forests when living creatures had flippers turning into limbs and scale to skin. The colors of this jungle-garden are violent,

Steaming jungle garden
An umbrella of gnarled fiddleleaf ficus gives an eerie ambience to the garden room that inspired the setting for Tennessee Williams's dark drama, Suddenly, Last Summer.

especially since it is steaming with heat after rain . . . there are harsh cries and sibilant hissings and thrashing sounds in the garden as if it were inhabited by beasts, serpents and birds, all of savage nature. . . ."

The importance of the room to the play was confirmed when the director of the 1959 movie version of the play asked to buy the Bultmans' wicker furniture. The family declined the offer. They did agree, nearly forty years later, to allow the Tennessee Williams Festival to use the Garden Room as the set for a production of the play.

The room and the garden just outside its rear doors were built by Johann Bultman's grandfather, Fred, who in the 1920s inherited the family's Garden District funeral business dating to the 1880s. It was Fred who collected the furniture and built the ornate iron stairs to connect the Garden Room with the second story of the house.

To decorate the garden outside, he used his collection of antique funerary art, most of which is in place today. After Fred Bultman, his daughter, Muriel Bultman Francis, an art collector, imposed her own sense of formality on the space. Then Johann and his wife became stewards of the property, and they have added their own layer.

On a hot, humid September morning, Johann Bultman toured the room and its outdoor garden, explaining along the way the fine

Moment of mourning
Beyond the room's French doors, an outdoor garden displays a cast-iron form of a woman in mourning and other funerary art gathered long ago by Fred Bultman from a deconsecrated cemetery in the central business district.

Bright garden ornament
Another of Fred Bultman's acquisitions is this nineteenth-century marble sculpture that blends the symbols of Christian Madonna and pagan earth goddess.

points of keeping the old fiddleleaf ficus trees healthy in their indoor habitat. The trees grow, in fact, through holes in the floor into the ground below. Bultman pampers them with fertilizer and by flipping on roaring box fans each morning to keep the white flies and scale from setting in.

The wicker furnishings are still here, arranged in circles around three large tables. Paintings, sculpture, and folk art are crammed into the room, along with a monumental sculpture cast in bronze by Bultman's father, Fritz, an abstract expressionist who for years taught art at Hunter College in New York.

More of Fritz Bultman's work is in the garden, surrounding a long swimming pool, itself hidden within a privacy screen of Savannah holly, sweet olive, cherry laurel, and crape myrtle. Dramatic details come from gardenias, hibiscus, and gingers, a wisteria vine that follows the trail of a two-story outdoor stairway, and enough salvia and milkweed to keep the butterflies on constant call.

Amid the plants stands a nineteenth-century marble sculpture of a woman with a star on her forehead—part Christian Madonna, part pagan earth goddess. Off to the left, a cast-iron figure of a mourning woman, her arms crossed, her face somber, presides over a fountain edged in acanthus leaves. Off to the right, a terra-cotta statue of Columbia balances the arrangement.

For more than seventy years, the family has slowly reconfigured the house and garden to suit the tastes of the residents of the moment. "It's a work in progress," Johann Bultman said, "and it will continue."

Glimpses of another time
Whitewashed wicker furnishings dappled in shade created by a forest of tropical plants were collected by Johann Bultman's grandfather, Fred.

Fran and George Villere
UPTOWN

Fran and George Villere bought one of the most spectacular mansions on St. Charles Avenue, a big powerful house on the city's finest street. For months, their high-profile renovation captured the attention of joggers, streetcar riders, and drivers who watched as the house became a perfectly tuned showplace. Unlike many of its neighbors, the Villere home is not at all in the delicate mode of southern architecture. Instead it is a fortress of hewn limestone in the brawny style of Richardson Romanesque.

Henry Hobson Richardson, born and reared in Louisiana, did not design the building, but he could have. Built in 1910 for an ambitious cotton baron, the house, designed by the venerable New Orleans architecture firm of Favrot and Livaudais, is perched atop a haughty terrace and wrapped in a border of majestic live oaks.

When the Villeres bought the property, the trees, behemoths by anyone's calculation, were in sore need of pruning, shaping, and fertilizing. As the trees were nurtured and revived, a task that continued for a year, the rest of the garden was wrought from fresh beginnings.

"The house was so strong from the street that it scared me," said Fran Villere, who knows her plants but prefers not to do much digging herself. "With its overgrown bushes and concrete walkways, I used to call it the haunted house before we bought it." But her husband had always wanted to live in the house so she conceded and sought ways to make it friendlier.

LEFT
Soft touch
Roses tangle above a garden gate, marking a homey corner of a garden that specializes in big, muscular plantings.

OPPOSITE
Quiet retreat on one of the city's busiest streets
The terrace and the swimming pool are landscaped with fragrant flowering plants such as dwarf gardenias, jasmines, and sweet olive.

To get the job done, the Villeres hired architect Leonard Salvato, a protégé of postmodernist Charles Moore, and René Fransen, a New Orleans–based landscape architect who has designed many dazzling gardens in the city's most rarefied neighborhoods.

Fransen advised the planting of comely pink sasanquas inside the iron fence along St. Charles Avenue, softening the edge from the street. He changed the burly marble approach to the front stairs, adding curves that diminished stiffness and heightened grandeur. Up the grassy terrace and around the deep front porch, he

added agapanthus, sago palms, azaleas, hawthorne, aspidistra, and calla lilies. Along the oak-sheltered drive to a porte-cochère, he put in fragrant gardenias and tucked orange-flowering clivias and a white-blooming native starbush into a ground cover of monkey grass.

During the three-year project, Fransen and Salvato proposed an addition that would make the garden one of a kind—a raised rear terrace graced with all the amenities of a small resort. Hiked off the ground by eight feet to allow for parking underneath, the terrace is adorned with a gazebo for entertaining, a plaza with a view of the avenue, and a long swimming pool, all meant to suggest a mood of quiet serenity in the midst of hectic city life.

Villere admits that embarking on the terrace took nerve, but she wanted to give Salvato and Fransen the opportunity to do something truly creative with the house. The project required ordering stone from the same Ohio quarry that Favrot and Livaudais used when the house was built, then finding a mason who could cut the stone to match the original. Four thousand pounds of blue slate were ordered for the terrace surface, along with tons of prime soil for plantings of hollies, palms, Japanese red maples, sweet olives, gardenias, fountain plants, and yesterday-today-and-tomorrow.

"It was very complicated to imagine the terrace but it was so interesting how they figured it all out," said Villere. "You feel like you're not there for the world to see, and yet you're in the great outdoors."

She walked though a pair of French doors that join a family room with the terrace and stepped along the flagstone toward the pool, pausing at a break in the planting allowing a

glimpse of a streetcar bustling by. Framing the view was a forty-foot tunnel of green formed by the live oaks and Chinese fan palms.

It was an exotic sight, even for Villere, who sees it every day but never takes it for granted. In flat-as-a-crepe New Orleans, where a rabid climate makes most gardens temporary, Villere's has permanence: stone and oaks and a grand view unlike any other, anywhere.

OPPOSITE
View toward the terrace
Arching live oaks, sagos, ground cover tucked with orange-flowering clivia, and other New Orleans standards form a powerful tunnel of green leading to the wall of the raised, rear-yard terrace.

RIGHT
Very private terrace
Landscape architect René Fransen placed lush firecracker vine, Xanadu philodendron, and sambac jasmine along the edges of the pool.

Sybil and Blair Favrot
FAUBOURG DELACHAISE

Inside a garden room
One of several screened
archways that pierce the
walls of the garden room
gives off to a stone terrace
and a path toward parterres
edged in boxwood.

RIGHT
Country-size garden
Borders, parterres, and vines
in dark green and white
stamp the sprawling garden
in the heart of Uptown with
the hallmarks of a southern
garden at summer's end.

"Time waits for no one," Sybil Favrot said,
cradling a glass of vanilla-spiked iced coffee
on the veranda of her country-size garden on
St. Charles Avenue. Before her, a vast lawn
stretched farther and farther, ending at a towering hedge of southern magnolias, hollies, and
catalpas that cast shadows over ribbons of
gardenias, boxwoods, and azaleas.

The lawn and hedge, as well as a parterre,
the crape myrtle allée, and a rose garden that
wrapped around the 1930s house, looked old
and settled. But most of it was new, proof of
Favrot's penchant for racing with time. After
she and her husband, Blair, bought the property,
she hit the ground running, ordering hundreds
of trees and shrubs of large proportions and
artfully planting them around the perimeter of
the property. In under six months she managed
to bring in a major garden with the mossy
patina of age.

"I really wanted to be able to enjoy the
garden right away—that's why I forged ahead
like that," said Favrot, who had at least three
landscape contractors out buying plants for her.
"I knew I wanted good southern plants like
sasanquas, gardenias, azaleas, sweet olives, and
the boxwoods. The basic Baby Hardie plants."

Baby Hardie, whose given name was
Dorothy, was the doyenne of genteel Uptown
landscaping through the 1940s, 1950s, and most
of the 1960s. A society girl herself with refined,
old-line taste, she shored up the notion of
moody gardens with dark green foliage, the
fragrance of gardenia and jasmine, and flowers

that were mostly white. The Favrots hired Hardie to help them with their first and second homes, both a mile or so from their present one.

"Whatever I know about gardening I learned from her," Favrot said of Hardie, who died in her eighties in the 1970s. "She had no formal training to my knowledge but she had a big influence on the way Uptown and the Garden District look now." Favrot recalled how Hardie would arrive at her home and ask for a chair to be brought out so she could sit and supervise as the holes were dug and the plants went in, being sure that new soil and fertilizer

were added and that everything was properly watered in.

Hardie was the one who encouraged Favrot's philosophy of picking plants that were "Old South," a category including the sturdy Lady Banksia roses that twine along a railing on the second-floor wall but not the dozens of tea roses that fill the bed off the garden room. When Favrot wanted to plant the roses in her first garden, Hardie told her no, she'd never have time to care for them.

"I immediately went out and bought seventy-five rose bushes," Favrot laughed, "and then I asked her, 'Baby, did you do that to challenge me or what?' She said 'I just wanted to see what would happen and it worked.'"

It was the size of the property on St. Charles that spurred Favrot to move from the house where she raised her children. Of course, one of the first steps she took was to enlarge the rose garden so she could enjoy its fragrance as she sat inside the garden room, and have flowers for her meticulously decorated home, a Classical Revival landmark designed in 1932 by architect Richard Koch. She renovated the interior with the same game plan that she used for the garden—first-rate and quick.

Asked why she decided to leave a perfectly fine home and move to such a big place at a time of life when many people choose to downsize, Favrot replied with a grin, "No fool like an old fool."

Michael and Basi Carbine

Walking through the gardens at Michael and Basi Carbine's home on Audubon Place feels something like pausing at a page in Edith Wharton's adventurous travelogue, *Italian Villas and Their Gardens.* Soaked in the dark leaves of parterres, hedges, and lawn and primped with a broad raised terrace and images of the Four Seasons and the Muses, the garden is soothing and edgy at the same time. The picturesque house, designed by New Orleans architect Emile Weil in 1910, always had a strong Italianate Revival character. But it became more so when the Carbines bought it and made a series of additions and alterations—especially the creation of a formal garden that could have been transported from somewhere on the outskirts of Rome.

It doesn't hurt that the house is nestled into a part of town dominated by the grandeur of Audubon Park, the campuses of Tulane and Loyola universities, and the broad St. Charles Avenue neutral ground. Known as the University Section, the area is a classic example of late nineteenth-century suburbanism. Audubon Place, a private cul-de-sac with a gatehouse, is one of its touchstones.

LEFT
First privacy, then parterres
The Carbines placed a wall and hedges along the rear of their property, separating it from a Tulane University service road. Then they installed a raised terrace and parterre worthy of an Italian villa.

Making a view
To add to the atmosphere, a classical marble statue was placed on an axis with the raised terrace.

Audubon Place, across St. Charles Avenue from the ceremonial entrance to Audubon Park, has plenty of pomp of its own. Its presence is announced by a Romanesque gateway designed by Thomas Sully. Beyond it, twenty-eight grand residences are arranged around a luxuriously landscaped neutral ground. Original property covenants require each house to have a forty-foot setback with no fences to interrupt it. With these deep lawns and the neutral ground a given, the Carbines, who bought the property in 1994, could spend their energy on the property's more private vistas. Key to the plan was relocating an oyster-shell driveway that wrapped around the rear of the house, a change that made way for a vast, uninterrupted landscape.

For hours, Michael Carbine said, he would peer out of windows on the second floor of the house, organizing the space in his mind, making notes as the light shifted and the seasons changed. First, a high wall was erected at the rear of the property, blocking out views of the traffic on a service road used by Tulane. Then a thick hedge of Eggleston holly was planted in front of the wall, followed by a stepped row of Japanese yew. Parterres and greenswards were created to break up the space, all set inside a backdrop of sculpted hedges, smart iron gates, and the impressive facades of the house and a matching garage and guesthouse.

Polishing the plan as he went, Carbine settled on the same palette of traditional evergreen plants that he has always favored: hollies and yews, boxwoods, camellias, gardenias, sweet

OPPOSITE
Garden getaway
At sundown, the terrace becomes a dining room where guests can enjoy the Carbines' perfectly primped garden filled with an inventory of old-fashioned evergreens that is kept small and choice.

LEFT
Spatial control
Carefully placed urns, planters, and parterres divide the big garden into small, intimate spaces.

olive, and grasses ranging from bermuda to zoysia. In spring and fall, white-flowering annuals are brought in as seasonal flourishes. To add to the atmosphere, a classic marble statue of plump toddlers playing music—a gift from Basi's garden-loving mother—was placed on an axis with a parterre and the raised terrace, grandly furnished and outfitted with drop

awnings that, when lowered, turn the space into a cozy outdoor den.

"The greens are so wonderful," said Carbine, looking at the garden from the terrace, presenting a view straight out of the pages of Wharton's book. "These are the things that grow for me in New Orleans. They're tried-and-true and I keep repeating them in different forms."

Thomas Lemann
UPTOWN

Ask lawyer Thomas B. Lemann to explain his sumptuous garden on Garfield Street and he might begin with praise for his magnificent pair of live oaks. If he is in the mood, he might even pull out their certificates of membership in the Live Oak Society, an honor bestowed on specimens of *Quercus virginiana* a hundred years or older. Known as the Martlet Oak and the Opinicus Oak—and perhaps no more than seedlings when New Orleans was new—the broad-spreading trees form the backbone of Lemann's carefully constructed landscape.

First there is Martlet Oak, hovering like a swan with unfurled wings over the formal entrance to Lemann's low-lying modernist home. Then there is Opinicus Oak, the centerpiece of a grand panoramic view that stretches along the opposite side of the house.

"The main attraction of the property was the land and the two big trees," said Lemann, looking out the glass wall of his living room at

Consider the aged oak
The curved limb of Opinicus Oak and the brick bench form a grand panorama that stretches across the front rooms of Thomas Lemann's home.

Collected works
Mounted on a brick pedestal, a sculpture by Paolo Boni called Glyph *is one of many artworks that dot the landscape.*

OPPOSITE

Serenity beyond
the library
To create a view from the
library, San Francisco
landscape architect Robert
Royston designed a stream
that flows down an artificial
incline into a pool of polished
stones. Toward the rear of
the garden, a hedge of pink
sasanquas brings winter
color to the garden.

Brick tunnel
Uccello, *a stone sculpture*
by Finnish artist Harry
Kivijarvi, marks the entrance
to a tunnel that connects
the main house with the
guest house.

the gargantuan limb of Opinicus, nearly dusting the ground in its long horizontal thrust from the trunk of the tree. "I've often said that we don't have any mountains or hills at all in New Orleans. We're all flat. The landscape is the trees—and the oak is the main tree."

When Lemann and his wife, Barbara, bought the property in the 1960s, it included a rambling Victorian house facing prestigious State Street. The Lemanns wanted to replace the old house with one that was contemporary in design, in large part so they could enjoy the animated spectacle of the oaks as they grew in stature and demonstrated their lovely seasonal changes. They hired the respected San Francisco landscape architect Robert Royston to site the house and to work in collaboration with New Orleans architect John Lawrence, who later became dean of the Tulane University School of Architecture. The two men worked as a team, combining the home and its grounds into an elegant urban compound.

Royston advised slipping the house between the oaks, allowing one to announce the main entrance and the other to provide a view from the other side of the house. To intensify the experience, a wall was built around the perimeter of the property, a device that ensured privacy, created atmosphere, and magnified the bewitching presence of the trees.

The design for the house provided a long bank of windows that gives off to a terrace covered by a series of overhead arches that frame views from inside. Steps lead from the terrace to a broad lawn, which, in turn, ends at a brick bench that tracks the curving path of an oak limb. From inside the dining room, the tree's massive trunk is the main attraction,

especially when the garden is lit at night. From inside the living room, the mammoth limb, hanging from the trunk like a freighter's mooring line, is the star of the show.

From the next room, a library where Lemann keeps his store of gardening books, the view switches from the dramatic oak to a quiet water garden. The garden features a stream that begins with a fountain at the far end and moves softly down an incline. "It's the only flowing stream in New Orleans—and the only artificial hill," said Lemann, whose curiosity about the natural world once prompted him to hire landscape architect James Fondren to teach him how to identify the predominant trees in New Orleans.

Over time, Lemann established a private arboretum of sorts in a walled garden room near the stream. There he grows many of the trees he admires—gingko, bald cypress, magnolia, a lucky nut he grew from seed he gathered in Jamaica, as well as a metasequoia, a deciduous conifer from China. His interest in trees has set him on travels throughout the world to measure the girths of champion trees. In Louisiana, he knows very well the Seven Sisters Oak, President of the Live Oak Society, with a girth of thirty-eight feet. He also knew the tree's predecessor, the Hahnville Oak, which was about 450 years old when it died. Not long ago, Lemann went to see the biggest tree in Louisiana—a bald cypress with a girth of more than fifty feet. Living deep inside the Tunica Swamp near Baton Rouge, the tree is estimated at 800 years old.

As for his own live oaks, Lemann thinks they are probably between 150 and 250 years old. "They're not the biggest in town by any means," he said. Some measure twenty-five feet; his trees are fourteen and seventeen.

Robert and Elizabeth Livingston
THE UNIVERSITY SECTION

Covered with an arbor thick with wisteria and honeysuckle, the second-story porch of Robert and Elizabeth Livingston's vintage craftsman-style cottage offers a spectacular view that presents itself in three stages. In the distance, the glazed tile rooftops of St. Charles Avenue mansions poke through the boughs of live oaks like mountains in the clouds. In the middle ground, a stand of bamboo soars upward for forty feet, its canes clanking in the wind, turning nature into music. Closer, beneath the porch, the Livingstons' garden spreads out like a colorful mosaic and invites a closer look.

Any serious gardener would readily comply.

Robert Livingston, a Zen master with a background in investment banking, is the gardener here. His wife, an artist, sometimes helps with composition, but for the most part she uses the garden as inspiration for her paintings. Robert, though, is there to work. And keeping thousands of flowering plants humming along is his pleasure.

In summer it is not unusual to find dramatic patches of six-foot-tall dahlias, bright blue lobelias, and angel's trumpets in beds that line the meandering path through the garden. Along the way, there are pots filled with bougainvillea, coreopsis, and impatiens in bright hues, and more beds lushly planted with hibiscus, oleander, dwarf hydrangea, crimson bottlebrush, bird-of-paradise, lavender buddleia, and other treats for winged wildlife.

OPPOSITE
Waterless whimsy
Dwarf papyrus skips
over the rim of a moss-
covered fountain.

ABOVE
View from the second-
story porch
Boughs from a live oak and
dramatic sprays of palms and
bamboo blur the elevated
vista of St. Charles Avenue's
handsome rooflines.

To nourish the completely organic garden, Livingston has three compost tumblers going full throttle outside the door to his potting shed. They provide him with heaps of rich soil that form the underpinnings of his super-charged landscape. But surely the most extravagant project Livingston has undertaken as a gardener involves the towering bamboo grove that guides a visitor into the heart of the garden. Livingston described the transformation of the onetime paved driveway: "We dug a trench two feet deep and ten feet wide and shoveled out all that heavy clay. I'd go over to Audubon Zoo every morning, get manure from the elephants and other animals, dump it in my pickup, drive home, and spread it all down around the bottom of the trench. I did that for weeks."

When the bed was ready, he drove to a nursery near Birmingham, Alabama, bought some prize bamboo, ferried it home through a ferocious rainstorm, and planted it. These days, the former driveway is a long grove of mixed bamboos, accessible by a soft pine-needle path that crunches underfoot. Along the way Livingston's bamboo collection reveals itself—henon, bory, golden bamboo, then a stretch of black bamboo, then the rare Sacred Bamboo of Bali.

An ardent plant gatherer, Livington scours local nurseries and garden shows, always looking for something new and exciting. When he can't find what he wants, he orders from his stash of mail-order catalogs.

From the second-story porch, it is possible to observe just about every inch of the thickly planted garden, including such alluring plants as Australian tree ferns, white cleome, and Tonkin cane.

"Every morning I stand on the porch and look at it as the dawn comes on," said Livingston. "That's the most magical time. Then I go down for a walk. The dew on the leaves glistens and then the sun starts hitting and the colors of the flowers slowly begin to pop out in the growing light."

Art Gardens

Travel just about anywhere in New Orleans and you'll find sculpture and greenery blended together in lovely compositions: Louis Armstrong snuggling his trumpet on the edge of a pond in Armstrong Park, General Beauregard astride his horse on a landscaped circle in front of City Park, Joan of Arc poised for battle in a leafy triangle in the French Quarter, Simon Bolívar, in full military regalia, posed on the neutral ground of Basin Street.

Urban vignettes such as these are public and there for everyone to see—showcased in parks large and small, along the grassy waterfront of the Mississippi River, the tree-shaded neutral grounds of the city's boulevards, and the stylish plazas in the central business district.

Other gardens with art are private and harder to discover—hidden away in backyards and courtyards and even on rooftops across the city. Often these are the creations of artists and art collectors who like to live amid their possessions. When they gaze out a window, they want to see their treasures framed and enhanced by foliage. When they walk through the garden, they want to experience it as a casual gallery alfresco.

When nineteenth-century gardens had sculptural elements, they were usually small and figural and made of stone or cast iron. Today, in a city proud of its creative edge, artworks on display tend to represent a wide range of local artists, often starting with celebrated sculptors

*Honoring Armstrong
A likeness of native son
Louis Armstrong (by artist
Elizabeth Catlett) takes center stage in Armstrong Park,
an expanse of green and
waterways and home to the
Mahalia Jackson Theatre
for the Performing Arts
and WWOZ, a radio station
specializing in local music.*

such as Enrique Alferez, Arthur Silverman, Lin Emery, John Scott, and Ida Kohlmeyer, who have helped make New Orleans a center of contemporary art in the Southeast. But that is one of the few things these gardens have in common. For the most part, they are the creations of owners who strive to blend the hard textures of stone, metal, and glass with the softer textures of trees, shrubs, and flowering plants.

One such garden was summoned from the remains of a neighborhood barroom that once served as a stopping-off point for five genera-tions of Uptowners. Another was built around a historic cottage designed by one of the city's finest late-nineteenth-century architects, Thomas Sully. Still another was carved into a swampy parcel of land on the edge of the river in a hard-to-find cranny of New Orleans called the Lower Coast of Algiers.

And so it goes, garden after garden. Each one different, each one offering a testimony on the rich possibilities of folding together art made in a studio and art made outdoors in a garden.

Art in the park
The classical facade of the New Orleans Museum of Art and the kinetic sculpture by New Orleans artist Lin Emery at its entrance contribute to the large collection of outdoor art placed throughout the 1,500-acre park.

Lucianne and Joe Carmichael
THE LOWER COAST OF ALGIERS

Recalling birds and bayous
A handmade pond is wrapped
in trees, and a leaf-covered
path is dotted with sculptures
by artist Larry Nevil
and metal herons titled
Honored Guests *by Joe*
and Lucianne Carmichael.

Part man, part nature. Think of this garden as an artwork in itself. Laid into an ancient eight-acre stretch of bottomland off River Road, it is the ultimate in contradictions: a sophisticated outdoor art gallery existing within the primal, critter-infested landscape of mossy Louisiana.

You would never guess as you passed the exclusive English Turn gated community that a place so offbeat as Gallery in the Woods could

lie near the end of the road at an otherworldly spot where the Mississippi River meets the land. It would, indeed, be easy to pass it by, marked as it is only by a small, fanciful metal sign.

On the road to the house, perched on a log, a limestone head of a man by sculptor Larry Nevil stares skyward. Near it, a figure of a woman in flight sways with the wind. Beyond, an oversized jardiniere, glazed pink and blue and aquamarine, pops into

view. And then comes the sight of the Carmichaels' house, carefully set between the water oaks, looking as if it, too, had emerged from an acorn.

Inside a long screened porch with a hanging swing and rockers, the Carmichaels are easily coaxed into talking about the watery heart of the garden that spreads out beyond the house—past a bog of ferns and iris and a cluster of rusted sculptures made by artist Paul Fowler from machine parts. The Carmichaels dug the pond soon after they bought the property. A promontory at one end was cultivated as a memorial garden to the Carmichaels' late son. The first piece of sculpture in the garden, meant to mark the memorial, was made of metal by sculptor Lin Emery. Step by step, more plantings and artworks and then benches were added to the path around the pond.

"The idea of an outdoor sculpture garden came slowly," said Lucianne Carmichael, an educator-turned-potter who moved to the woods

Seamless transitions
A generous screened porch makes a gentle connection between the comfortable interior of the Carmichaels' home and the lush landscape outside.

OPPOSITE

Art and the wild

A retrospective of the
work of sculptor-painter
Larry Nevil was displayed
throughout the woodsy landscape of the Carmichaels'
home and gallery.

RIGHT

Sign of welcome

At the beginning of the road
to the Carmichaels' property,
a cheery sculpture by
Connecticut artist Karen
Rossi marks the entry.

so she could find quiet and inspiration for her own work. "Of course the beginning of every-thing was the property—its feeling of specialness and the beauty and naturalness. You almost didn't have to do anything to it at all. It was a perfect work of natural art."

Out on the leaf-paved path, the air is moist and cool and the morning sky is gray and threatening. One step leads to another artwork, also by Nevil, a former schoolteacher who recently had a show of his paintings and sculptures at the gallery. Birds speed from one treetop to the next and dive toward the underbrush. Foghorns from ships on the river heading to the Gulf of Mexico boom through the humid air.

Yards of spider webs, wrapped around one tree and then the next, form a gleaming screen between the path and the pond. Golden weaver spiders go about their business, sharing their territory with thousands of dewdrops. Below, solitary leaves dangle on spider-made strands, glimmering like tiny mobiles as they turn in perpetual motion.

"This is a wonderful place to live, but this subtropical climate is hard," said Lucianne. "The things that we human beings put in here just wait to be eaten or grown on or rained on. It's almost a constant struggle between us and the environment to try to negotiate how we're both going to make it."

Near the end of the path, a glazed platter decorated with big-eyed fish stands on a log, its bowl filled with larvae, water, and leaves. It was made by Carmichael, a friendly gesture to the wildlife that shares the Gallery in the Woods with her, her husband, and the art.

Merce and Arthur Silverman
UPTOWN

When Merce Silverman set her sights on buying a crusty Uptown barroom called Graffagnino's and turning it into a home, her husband, physician-turned-sculptor Arthur Silverman, had his doubts about the project. They had a perfectly fine home a mile or so away, he argued, and, unlike the barroom, the home they had occupied for twenty years was not in need of a total overhaul. But his wife could not be dissuaded.

"I'm a frustrated architect and I'd been looking for a long time—without Artie's knowledge," she said with a wink, facing a kitchen window that gave way to a stylish garden filled with her husband's bold sculptures. The old house was nice, she said, but it didn't

Rustle of bamboo
Vaughn Banting, the designer of the Silvermans' garden, put in a small stand of bamboo to evoke the tradition of Japanese gardening, a minimal approach perfectly compatible with Silverman's spare sculpture.

LEFT
Sumptuous views
The living room is surrounded by views of the sculpture garden with its gravel paving and array of tropical plants such as Chinese fan palm, bamboo, and bird-of-paradise.

Covered walkway
Strong plants echo Arthur
Silverman's powerful
sculptures arranged along
a walk covered by an arc of
aluminum slats, a sculptural
approach to a functional
need for shade and privacy.

consisted of the building where the bar was, a garage, a small yard carpeted with oyster shells, and a narrow side alley.

Without tearing anything down, the Silvermans created a small, private compound, divorced from the street and focused inward. Constructed to meet at a right angle on the corner, the walls of the building enclosed the property on two sides and afforded a good deal of privacy. Elsewhere, sheets of corrugated metal fencing were installed to complete the enclosure. Along the alley, a long arc of aluminum slats designed by Silverman and fabricated by his righthand man, Thomas Charrier, was used to create a covered walkway. Meanwhile, the interior of the building was reconfigured so that most of the main rooms faced either the rear yard or the alley. Generous squares of glass framed views from the living room, dining room, and kitchen, connecting them to the garden.

To create the landscape and to help place about twenty pieces of large-scale metal sculpture in it, the Silvermans turned to Vaughn Banting, a noted landscape designer whose work is informed by his knowledge of bonsai and the garden traditions of Japan. "It's Vaughn's garden," said Arthur Silverman, heading outside toward a shimmering stainless steel sculpture standing beside a tall bird-of-paradise plant. "Originally he thought as I did that the emphasis would be on the sculpture, but he just kept adding plants as it seemed appropriate."

Whenever Silverman would bring a new artwork to the garden, Banting helped position it and sometimes reconsidered the plantings. He relied on tropicals and perennials with strong architectural forms. Bamboo was one of his choices, along with shell ginger and sweet olive, Louisiana iris,

ABOVE AND OPPOSITE
Art in detail
Silverman's work can be found in his own garden, as well as in public and private spaces throughout Louisiana and beyond.

work as a backdrop for his art. In a nutshell, the house and the garden were separate and distinct, and Merce wanted them to be one.

Graffagnino's would solve the problem, she insisted, and her husband came to agree. What they had to work with was a popular neighborhood hangout on Calhoun Street that had been in operation since the 1920s. The property

dwarf mondo grass, agapanthus, and golden ray.

The strong shapes of the plants echo Silverman's powerful geometric sculptures, usually rendered in metal and frequently fashioned in tetrahedrons. Sheltering the landscape like an oversized umbrella is an eccentric old live oak that reinforces the garden's sense of intimacy and serenity.

Merce Silverman points out that the garden has taken on the flavor of a French Quarter courtyard, borrowing the feeling of enclosure and reinterpreting the form with Asian sensibilities. It was Banting's suggestion, for instance, to use gravel for paving instead of grass, flagstone, or brick. "The gravel is a Japanese idea," she said. "Otherwise you'd be standing on grass and it wouldn't be the same experience as standing on this surface and looking at the sculpture." The absence of pathways, Banting figured, makes the garden a blank slate, like the walls of an art gallery.

With this notion in mind, very little was planted in the ground. Instead, large containers are carefully placed throughout the garden. For the scale he wanted, Banting used oversized birdbath bowls and got just the right effect.

What the three have created is a one-of-a-kind sculpture garden that is alluring from any perspective. From an upholstered seat at the dining room table, the view is tightly fixed on Silverman's outdoor gallery. From the living room and the kitchen, the scope is larger, taking in a clustered still life of sculptures. But the full effect is best viewed during a walk along the exotic sculpture alley formed by Silverman's aluminum arc where the architecture, the sculpture, and the plants all work together to form a synergistic whole, just the way Merce Silverman hoped they would.

Sandra and Richard Freeman
UPTOWN

Roses, art, and architecture are at the heart of Sandra and Richard Freeman's graceful garden on Henry Clay Avenue, a quiet street cuddled close to St. Charles Avenue and Audubon Park. Located on a corner lot, the garden wraps around the couple's large, graceful cottage, the work of the esteemed late-nineteenth-century New Orleans architect Thomas Sully.

The property still retains the feeling of the 1890s when the house was built in a developing upriver section of town that was more of a rural hamlet than an extension of a high-spirited city. In those days, Audubon Park was wild and overgrown, providing a mysterious backdrop for the pretty houses that dotted its perimeter.

When they bought the house in the early 1990s, the Freemans determined to make it into a pastoral setting for the artworks they had collected over the course of thirty-five years. They wanted to transform the property in a way that would allow them to display their sculptures and paintings with ease, arranging them to their best advantage in an architecturally important house. The solution was to build a large transparent room that would overlook the garden and its sculpture, while permitting views from the garden into the art-filled house.

Architect Pio Lyons designed a glass room that echoes the curving form of the front porch created by Sully. Then artist Mario Villa designed copper palm and palmetto fronds to decorate the uppermost exterior edge of the room, as well as the garden's portal—an iron gate and fence with cutouts of half-moons and horses.

Passage through the gate, softened by a lacy bower of rambling roses, reveals a sculpture of a mother fleeing with her infant child. Titled *Vietnam*, it is the work of Enrique Alferez, an artist whose sculpture for the Works Progress Administration in the 1930s molded the character of many New Orleans public spaces, including 1,500-acre City Park.

"It's a very strong piece of sculpture," said Sandra Freeman, who mounted a large exhibit of Alferez's work at Longue Vue House and Gardens before he died in 1999 at the age of ninety-eight. "I love his work and I loved him."

Inside the glass room—an art gallery, really—brightly colored sculptures by New Orleans artist Ida Kohlmeyer vie for attention with artworks by George Dureau and Robert Gordy. They sit comfortably alongside French antiques and 1950s modernist furniture. At night the room can be doused in light, giving it the look of a surreal movie screen from the darkened garden. Or it can work the other way around, when the room is darkened and the lights in the garden come on.

As much a lover of plants as she is of art, Sandra Freeman asked local rose authority Eddie Sanchez to help her establish a collection of climbing, rambling, and shrub roses. More

OPPOSITE
Art inside and out
A new garden room filled with paintings and sculpture repeats the graceful curve of the front portico at the Freemans' home, designed by prominent nineteenth-century architect Thomas Sully.

RIGHT
Mother in flight
Vietnam, *a sculpture by Enrique Alferez, encourages visitors to slow down and enjoy the Freemans' outdoor art collection.*

Artful transition
Gates designed by New
Orleans sculptor Mario Villa
and laced with roses invite
visitors into the Freemans'
unique wrap-around garden.

OPPOSITE
Extension of the garden
Chinese fan palms and
butterfly gingers, along with
exuberant metal palmetto
and palm fronds by Mario
Villa, edge the garden
room—which itself is part
of the sculpture garden.

OPPOSITE RIGHT
Blooming their heads off
Canes of fire-engine red
Dortmund, a hybrid of
Rosa kordesii, weave
through the wrought-iron
fence, creating their own
dazzling piece of Sandra
Freeman's rose garden.

than a dozen varieties are represented, including a spectacular red-blooming Dublin Bay that tumbles over an arbor and a profusion of Dortmund, Clair Matin, and Sally Holmes that twine along the front fence.

With the help of landscape designer Chris Fischer, Freeman established an oval patio off the glass room, a curving path of disconnected concrete squares, and an herb garden. Over the years, an array of specimen plants such as giant tibouchina, blue spiral ginger, and montbretia have been brought in to give the garden depth. But the stars of the show remain as Freeman intended—the art, the architecture, and the roses.

Steve Coenen
FAUBOURG MARIGNY

In Faubourg Marigny, a neighborhood just a bit downriver from the French Quarter, Steve Coenen gardens around a simple, blue-collar cottage with a rebelliousness that comes from too much immersion in the classic New Orleans style. A professional gardener with a degree in landscape architecture from Louisiana State University, Coenen works for clients who generally want a tried-and-true, moonlight-and-magnolias garden look. But when he gets home he tosses quiet good taste out the window and orchestrates a garden that can best be described in one word: bombastic.

The first clue that Coenen's garden is out of step is on the facade of the house, where he has trained a heraldic swag of English ivy to drape around campy bumper stickers, collections of bowling trophies, and a lone cow's skull. The scene is completed by a stand of bald cypress trees, some prickly pyracantha, and tufts of red-flowering bleeding heart.

But Coenen, a tap dancer by avocation, saves his most dramatic flourishes for the rear garden, where he arranges all manner of high-style junk he picks up along garbage truck routes and from clients offering hand-me-downs. Set into small tableaux with a bounty of bright and flamboyant plants illuminated from dusk on with overhead strands of lights, the garden is like a stage set for a slapstick musicale. A visitor can do nothing more than leave worries at the door, take a seat on the covered porch, and have a rollicking good time.

When Coenen bought the house twenty

years ago, the property was anything but funny. The previous owner had put boards and chain-link fencing over the windows and encouraged a gloomy foreboding to set in. As for the garden, there was one magnificent fig tree, and the rest was a gnarled wasteland of neglect. Coenen kept the grandfatherly fig tree and ripped everything else out.

He created his garden solely from his vast store of orphaned plants and abandoned kitsch, arranging them into woodsy walkways and zany zigzags. Among his greatest treasures are a filigreed chandelier (wired and hanging from a tree) pried from a trash pile outside the home of Bourbon Street entertainer Chris Owens, a covey of headless stone creatures (now the centerpiece of a burbling fountain), and tens of thousands of broken porcelain shards (encrusted by Coenen into the surface of cement planters).

LEFT
Sinking ship
Steve Coenen modeled his rear porch after an upside-down boat, allowing an unencumbered view of the hand-me-downs he uses to decorate his garden. The collection includes odd pots, discarded chandeliers, and chunks of rusty iron, along with bowling balls and stepping-stones he covers with broken bits of pottery and porcelain.

OPPOSITE
Observation deck
Within the shelter of the porch, the garden in late winter unfolds in stages. The foreground and middle ground can be easily seen, but to experience the attractions beyond, a visitor must wade through the clutter. Coenen likes objects that are round or curved, and he likes everything to have either a lightbulb or a flowering plant in it.

"The garden just evolved from gathering up things that nobody else wanted and finding a place to plug them in," said Coenen, drinking iced tea and rocking on the porch that looks out over his thirty-by-forty-foot garden. "Most of the trees came out of some of the best gardens in town, and all the crazy stuff hanging from trees comes from the garbage heap."

Spread throughout this eccentric glade are thickly planted mounds of flowering annuals such as petunias, begonias, impatiens, nasturtiums, and sweet alyssum in the loudest of colors. To eliminate any bare spots, Coenen throws around at least five pounds of mixed seeds each season.

In the summer, the place comes alive with noisy blue jays harvesting figs. Through the year, turtles come and go and colonies of frogs main-tain permanent residence. To celebrate the end of summer, Coenen likes to construct a tiny forest of staked-and-pruned orange and yellow marigolds in a bed with a sphere of frosted glass in the center. Another regular feature is a box-wood parterre laid out like the aisles, nave, and spires of a Gothic cathedral.

Overhead, an umbrella of fragrant sweet olives, banana shrub, kumquats, dogwoods, cherry laurels, and assorted camellias deploy shade, color, and fragrance. Some towering slash pines remind Coenen of his boyhood on a farm in north Louisiana where he fell in love with gardening.

Coenen's sharp eye and his outlandish sense of style have made a memorable garden from practically nothing, except what he proudly claims as his strongest suit: the instincts of a junkyard dog.

House Museums

Occupying the territory between the grand green spaces that define New Orleans' public side and the personal gardens that reveal its private side are a handful of house museums with gardens open throughout the year (see details on page 202). For the price of admission, a visitor can tour the properties, often with a guide schooled in the history of the house, its architecture, and some of the fine points of the garden.

Generations of New Orleanians have traipsed through these gardens, admiring the soft old brick, smelling the sweet fragrances, and picking up bits of knowledge as they go. Later they may come to use what they learned to inform decisions for their own backyards, porches, and patios, thereby keeping the city's gardening history vibrant and alive.

For visitors to New Orleans, the museums provide a way of learning about the origins of the city's horticulture and landscape design—how the home and the garden were thought of as one and how they endured together over time.

The French Quarter has the lion's share of house-and-garden museums. Some pay more attention to the gardens and the plantings than others do, but each is worth a visit. The Ursuline Convent, established by the Sisters of St. Ursula, the first Catholic nuns to settle in New Orleans, has an old parterre garden, as

OPPOSITE
Graceful formality
Grand live oaks, swaths of woodland ferns, and beds of roses are hallmarks of the garden at Longue Vue House and Gardens.

Carefully clipped parterre
From the attic of the Beauregard-Keyes House, the garden filled with old Louisiana plants is revealed in all its symmetry.

well as an expansive new garden with herbs, roses, and sculptural homages to a group of significant nuns—all overseen by a priest and a prominent local chef. Across Chartres Street from the convent, the Beauregard-Keyes House, built in the 1820s, is noted for its reconstructed nineteenth-century parterre garden as well as for its handsome courtyard. A block away on Royal Street, Gallier House Museum has a courtyard reconstructed from the hand-drawn plans of its architect-owner, James Gallier Jr. Toward Canal Street on Royal Street, the Williams Residence, home of the founders of the Historic New Orleans Collection, a vast archival library, offers a garden designed by Richard Koch, a pioneering local architect who helped spawn the city's preservation movement in the 1930s. On nearby St. Louis Street, the Hermann-Grima House offers an ornamental parterre restored by Baton Rouge landscape historian Suzanne Turner.

Outside of the Quarter, the Pitot House on Bayou St. John, home in 1810 to the first mayor of New Orleans, hints at what an early suburban garden might have been like. A few miles away,

on the edge of Orleans Parish, Longue Vue House and Gardens, the twentieth-century estate of philanthropists Edith and Edgar Stern, represents a prominent example of the work of landscape architect Ellen Biddle Shipman.

Beyond the gardens of house museums, private gardens throughout the city are shown through tours sponsored by dozens of neighborhood groups. Most of these tours are in the spring and fall, when the weather is pleasant and the gardens are at their best. In addition, there are ongoing walking tours of the French Quarter and the Garden District. During weekends in early April and October, the New Orleans Botanical Garden in City Park mounts garden shows that bring out thousands of plant lovers from throughout the region. Growers of choice exotics and natives come from around the Southeast to sell their plants. Along with the sales, there are talks by plant experts on an array of topics that can range from southern garden design to old-fashioned roses to hardy bulbs and organic gardening.

For garden lovers, these places and events are among the best attractions the city has to offer.

Beauregard-Keyes House
THE FRENCH QUARTER

OPPOSITE
*Tucked neatly
into its surrounding
Like so many components
of the French Quarter,
the garden at the
Beauregard-Keyes House
is a modest pleasure with
lots of history behind it.*

RIGHT
*Primped parterre
A centerpiece fountain
surrounded by a handsome
parterre garden can be
enjoyed from afar by
passersby on Chartres and
Ursulines Streets or at
closer range by visitors to the
Beauregard-Keyes House.*

On cool mornings in the spring and fall, the unmistakable tealike fragrance of sweet olive at the Beauregard-Keyes House blows through the Lower French Quarter like an aromatic siren. Follow the scent and you'll end up at a pristine parterre garden, enclosed by an elegant brick wall. Rising above the wall are carefully groomed magnolias and white-flowering crape myrtles; piercing the wall are lacy squares of open iron grillwork. The view into the garden is like looking through the opening of a spun-sugar Easter egg—the sweet olives are pruned like baby's rattles, a tiered cast-iron fountain cascades with tumbling water, and clipped boxwood makes the perfect counterpoint for fanciful old-fashioned plants.

If that is not enough, climb the stairs to the Beauregard-Keyes House and sign up for a guided tour that begins at the top of each hour.

Named for its two most famous residents—Confederate General Pierre Gustave Toutant Beauregard and novelist Frances Parkinson Keyes—the house, with all its windows and doors, plays prettily to the parterre garden on the side and the paved courtyard garden at the rear.

A prolific writer whose best-known novel is *Dinner at Antoine's,* Keyes moved into the house in the early 1940s. At the time, it was in the hands of preservationists who had thwarted a proposal to replace it with a macaroni factory. Keyes was intent on restoring the house. "If not to its erstwhile grandeur, at least to some semblance of its original dignity and symmetry," she wrote in the foreword to *Madame Castel's Lodger,* a novel about General Beauregard created while she lived in the house.

Keyes hired architect Richard Koch, who had a keen understanding of the relationship between a home and its garden. He had come to know Beauregard House and other prominent Louisiana buildings during his time as the state's director of the federally sponsored Historic American Building Survey. As part of the restoration plan, Koch refurbished the slave quarters and devised a design for the ruined courtyard, calling for flagstone paving, planting beds with brick edging, and a centerpiece fountain.

Keyes found what she called the fountain of her dreams—made of iron and topped by a wistful cherub—in the yard of a New England

guesthouse. "It was obviously not working and, I gathered, not highly prized," she wrote in a magazine piece. "I boldly rang the doorbell and asked the owner of the house if she would care to sell the fountain."

A decade later, Keyes and Koch began planning the parterre, a much more complicated venture since it required demolishing the building next door and re-establishing a garden that had been there in the 1860s.

The old plan called for four quadrants of rectangles with a round fountain in the middle. As work proceeded, members of the Garden Study Club of New Orleans found historically appropriate plants and gathered them for the garden. Boxwood defined the edges of the parterre, forming beds that were filled with Asian jasmine and spring-blooming snowflakes. Southern magnolias were planted on the edges, along with sasanqua, pomegranate, naked lady, loquats, kumquats, and more.

Along the brick wall, two marble plaques attest to the long history of the garden and the people who have cared for it. One is to Veronica Hornblower, Keyes' secretary who died while the garden was under construction. The other, salvaged from a demolished cemetery near Canal Street, marked the tomb of the woman who made the original garden. Faded by time, the inscription reads "Anais A. Merle, née Phillippon, épouse de John A. Merle, décédée le 8 janvier 1847."

Light and shadow
A tiered fountain forms the animated heart of the garden, reconstructed by Frances Parkinson Keyes in the 1950s.

Ursuline Convent
THE FRENCH QUARTER

The Rev. Alvin J. O'Reilly is the keeper of what is thought to be the oldest French colonial building in the Mississippi Valley, the Ursuline Convent, built in 1734. An experienced hand at upgrading property belonging to the Catholic Church in New Orleans, Father O'Reilly moved into a small house behind the convent in the early 1990s and got busy caring for the historic complex. Among his plans was the tilling of a broad swath of land, which had been used for years as a parking lot. The idea was to evoke the eighteenth-century garden where the nuns once raised herbs to treat the sick and vegetables and fruits to feed the orphans of the new French colony. About as long as half a football field and twice as wide, the garden occupies a generous chunk of land considering the compressed lots of the French Quarter.

After a lot of stops and starts, the garden is taking on its own idiosyncratic character. It's not the historic restoration that some preservationists and gardeners in the city wished for. But it is a garden that displays the vision of O'Reilly and his gardening sidekick, French Quarter chef Horst Pfeiffer. For O'Reilly, the space has become a way to honor the Ursuline order; for Pfeiffer, it has become a lavish herb garden where he grows rosemary, basil, thyme, and dozens of other herbs for Bella Luna, his nearby restaurant on the riverfront.

After Sunday Mass one morning in early fall, O'Reilly, a tall, ruddy man who bears a resemblance to John Wayne, embarked on a tour of his garden. He started out at a small foyer in the hand-hewn convent building and made his way to a large outdoor mosaic he commissioned, depicting the Ursuline nuns praying for the survival of the city during a devastating fire that all but destroyed the French Quarter in 1788 and, later, during the Battle of New Orleans.

Past the mural, the garden splits into large grassy rectangles surrounded by beds of antique roses such as Duchesse de Brabant, Maman Cochet, and Souvenir de Malmaison, and large rectangles planted with Pfeiffer's crops. On the riverside wall, a shrine to Our Lady of Prompt Succor set among citrus trees and angel's trumpet forms the centerpiece of the garden. Fanned around it like figures in a Christmas tableau are O'Reilly's most recent additions to the garden— life-size marble likenesses of Frances Xavier Cabrini, the first American saint and a resident of New Orleans, along with Philippine Rose Duchesne, Katherine Drexel, Cornelia Peacock Connelly, and Henriette Delille, all of whom visited the convent and made great contributions to the city of New Orleans and all of whom are in line for sainthood.

"The idea is to honor these women," said O'Reilly. "I don't know if there's another place in the United States to have an association with five nuns either canonized or in the process." The sculptures, the roses, the herbs, the mosaic, and even the small pond evoke a time when women living within these walls helped to establish a new city in the New World.

Slice of the garden
Herb beds created and maintained by a French Quarter chef, profusions of perennials and tropicals, statues and towering date palms help define the garden masterminded by Father O'Reilly.

Longue Vue House and Gardens

NEW ORLEANS

In the 1940s, when the gardens at Longue Vue were young, it was not unusual for their creator, Ellen Biddle Shipman, to sit down with her pencils in the sunny salon of her clients, Edith and Edgar Stern, and proceed to rework old planting schemes. With eight acres of gardens to keep on track, Shipman never tired of primping and expanding her designs for the lavish estate.

The couple trusted Shipman so completely, in fact, that in the late 1930s they agreed to her proposal to hire architects William and Geoffrey Platt of New York to design a new house that would put the gardens at better advantage. To make way for the project, the Sterns moved the mansion they had built in 1923 to an empty lot down the way and sold it.

Longue Vue became known for its elegant series of garden rooms designed by Shipman, a New Yorker who started out with a little cottage garden in New Hampshire and wound up fashioning "Country Place" landscapes for wealthy Americans with names like Seiberling, Duke, and Dupont. Shipman's design studio in Manhattan, which employed only women, was responsible for more that six hundred major gardens across the country. Most of them have been lost and some are partly lost. Longue Vue is considered among the most intact examples of her work. A recent resurgence of interest in Shipman has helped attract more then fifty thousand visitors a year to Longue Vue, which Edith Stern, heiress to a Sears Roebuck fortune, turned over to a private foundation in the late 1960s.

Visitors come to see the majestic allée of live oaks that frame the main entrance to the Classical Revival house, wrapped in a lovely cloak of green spaces with evocative names such as the Pan Garden, the Wild Garden, the Kitchen Garden, and the Wall Garden. The Spanish Court, a long stone-and-brick promenade lined with splashing fountains, was added after Shipman's death in the 1950s and designed by her friend William Platt. In the late 1990s, a children's garden called the Discovery Garden was built in a place that Shipman had reserved for a greenhouse, a cutting garden, and a nursery.

For the most part, Edith Stern followed the spirit of Shipman's ambitious design, but after she died in the 1970s the gardens drifted toward a regimen of low-cost maintenance that obscured their original style. Picturesque walls and whimsical garden structures needed repair. Throughout the garden, a canopy of maturing shade trees edged out the jaunty flowering shrubs, perennials, and annuals that were a trademark of Shipman's spirited style.

Bothered by the deterioration, several of the Sterns' grandchildren contributed money to fund a restoration and management plan for the gardens, especially the ailing Wild Garden that Shipman designed with Caroline Dormon, Louisiana's pioneering advocate for native plants. Always a favorite of Edith Stern's, the Wild Garden contains a striking brick dovecote, a naturalistic pond, and a winding path carpeted in pine straw. The garden has luxuriant longleaf pines and bald cypress, along with a large collection

Unfolding in stages
Layers of roses, parterres, and oaks lead to the smooth turf of the adjacent New Orleans Country Club.

OPPOSITE
Allée of oaks
A canopy of live oaks covers
the drive from the main
entrance of the house, past
a gardener's cottage and out
to shady Bamboo Road.

RIGHT
Inside and out
The second-floor portico
with its long view of the
Spanish Court gives off to
a room where Edith and
Edgar Stern liked to confer
over morning coffee with
their landscape architect,
Ellen Biddle Shipman.

FAR RIGHT
On the green
One side of the house was
designed to resemble stately
Shadows-on-the-Teche in
New Iberia, Louisiana.
The view takes in an unin-
terrupted expanse of the
golf course at the New
Orleans Country Club.

FOLLOWING SPREAD
Plant with a past
Yesterday-today-and-
tomorrow, a native of South
America, was probably
introduced in New Orleans
around 1840. Its rich
fragrance and violet blooms,
which turn to white over two
days, make it an ongoing
favorite in gardens throughout the city.

The result of a long and congenial partnership
between the Sterns and Shipman, the property
shows what talent, enthusiasm, a generous
pocketbook, and a good working relationship
can achieve. The Sterns liked to call Shipman
"Lady Ellen, the godmother of Longue Vue,"
and even installed a bronze plaque in the Pan
Garden to praise her talents. Their admiration
for her was undoubtedly an important secret to
the garden's success.

"I am just writing to tell you how much we
enjoyed your visit, as always," Edgar Stern wrote
to Shipman in the 1930s, "and what a pleasure it
was to be able to sit down and discuss with you
at leisure the joy that we have every day in this
beautiful house and garden for which we are so
eternally indebted to you."

of Louisiana irises and native crinums. In an
effort to restore the garden to the sunny place it
once was, dozens of mature shade trees were
recently removed and smaller flowering trees
were brought in to replace them, a move that
denuded the landscape and stirred a controversy
between those who admired the garden in its
naturalized state and others who wanted to
recapture Shipman's earlier design scheme.

That dispute aside, the twentieth-century
estate created for the Sterns can easily hold
its own amid all of the compelling nineteenth-
century garden attractions in New Orleans.

Acknowledgments

THANKS TO THE MANY GARDENERS and garden ramblers, nursery owners and plant propagators, landscape designers, botanists, native-plant devotees, and wildlife watchers who contributed their knowledge and encouragement to *The Gardens of New Orleans.* The authors and photographer especially thank the following people who generously told the stories of their gardens and allowed them to be photographed: Doris and Ralph Cadow, Lucy Burnett, Barbara and Wayne Amedée, Bill Huls, Harry Worrell, George Dureau, Nancy Monroe and Jim Amoss, Stephen Scalia and Milton Melton, Mathilde and Prieur Leary, Betty DeCell, Julia Reed, Lolis Elie and Lisa Fuller, Luis and Dianna Guevara, Molly Reily, Eugénie and Ersy Schwartz, Charlotte and Jean Seidenberg, Henrietta Hudson, Geraldine and Willie Veal, Louis Aubert, Tim Trapolin, Malcolm and Alicia Heard, Johann and Bethany Bultman, Fran and George Villere, Sybil and Blair Favrot, Michael and Basi Carbine, Thomas Lemann, Robert and Elizabeth Livingston, Lucianne and Joe Carmichael, Merce and Arthur Silverman, Sandra and Richard Freeman, and Steve Coenen. We would also like to thank the Rev. Alvin J. O'Reilly of the Ursuline Convent and Marion Chambon of Beauregard-Keyes House.

Among those who opened our eyes to the wonders of gardening and helped us understand were Tran Asphrodites, Richard Barnes, Robert Becker, Douglas Bourgeois, Bob Brzuszek, Rose Buras, Barry Clark, Ella Cole, Marion Drummond, Bill Fontenot, René Fransen, Christopher Friedrichs, Karin Giger, Dan Gill, John Harris, Alicia Heard, Margie Jenkins, Jessie and Richard Johnson, John Mayronne, Richard McCarthy, Neil Odenwald, John Parrott, Robert Reich, Charlotte Seidenberg, Rosemary Sims, Paul Soniat, Melinda Taylor, Genevieve Trimble, Lee Wallace, and Wayne Womack.

Lake Douglas acknowledges the helpful comments and suggestions of John Lawrence and the enduring support of his wife, Debbie delaHousaye.

Jeannette Hardy would like to thank Jamaica Kincaid, whose writings in *The New Yorker* first sparked her curiosity about gardeners. She would also like to express her gratitude to Elizabeth Cole, Malcolm and Alicia Heard, Elizabeth Mullener, and Mimi Read, who kindly read drafts of the garden profiles in this book, and to Susan Larson, book editor of *The Times-Picayune,* who patiently nudged her into the book-writing world. Hardy is forever appreciative to her parents, Jeannette and Emanuel Gottlieb, and to her son, Zeph Hardy, for his optimism and encouragement. And to her husband, Bill Grady, who read every word and was, as always, the soul of patience.

Richard Sexton would like to acknowledge the generous assistance of the following establishments in granting access to their premises for the purpose of photographing specific subjects for this book: Gallier House, the Andrew Jackson Hotel, and the Presbytere. The administrations of the following public gardens graciously permitted and facilitated the taking of photographs on their grounds: Beauregard-Keyes House, Longue Vue House and Gardens, City Park, the New Orleans Botanical Garden, and Jackson Brewery.

House Museums Open to the Public

Beauregard-Keyes House
1113 Chartres Street
New Orleans, LA 70116
504-523-7257

Gallier House
1118-1132 Royal Street
New Orleans, LA 70116
504-525-5661

Hermann-Grima House
820 St. Louis Street
New Orleans, LA 70112
504-525-5661

Historic New Orleans Collection
533 Royal Street
New Orleans, LA 70130
504-523-4662

Longue Vue House and Gardens
7 Bamboo Road
New Orleans, LA 70124
504-488-5488

Pitot House
1440 Moss Street
New Orleans, LA 70119
504-482-0312

Ursuline Convent
1100 Chartres Street
New Orleans, LA 70116
504-529-3040

Further Reading

Beales, Peter. *Classic Roses.* New York: Henry Holt and Company, 1997.

Bender, Steve, ed. *The Southern Living Garden Book.* Birmingham, Ala.: Oxmoor House, 1998.

Brown, Clair A. *Louisiana Trees and Shrubs.* Baton Rouge: Claitor's Publishing Division, 1972.

Cable, George W. *The Amateur Garden.* New York: Charles Scribner's Sons, 1914.

Christovich, Mary Louise, et al. *New Orleans Architecture,* Vols. I–VIII. New Orleans: Pelican Press, 1971–1997.

Delahanty, Randolph. *Randolph Delahanty's Ultimate Guide to New Orleans.* San Francisco: Chronicle Books, 1998.

Douglas, William Lake. "Cultural Determinants in Landscape Architectural Typologies: Plants and Gardens in New Orleans from Colonial Times to the Civil War." *Journal of Garden History,* April–June, 1997.

Druitt, Liz. *The Organic Rose Garden.* Dallas: Taylor Publishing Company, 1996.

Federal Writers' Project of the Works Progress Administration for the City of New Orleans. *New Orleans City Guide.* Cambridge, Mass.: Houghton Mifflin Company, 1938.

Fontenot, William R. *Native Gardening in the South.* Carencro, La.: Prairie Basse Publications, 1992.

Gill, Dan, and Joe White. *Louisiana Gardener's Guide.* Franklin, Tenn.: Cool Springs Press, 1997.

Heard, Malcolm. *French Quarter Manual: An Architectural Guide to New Orleans' Vieux Carré.* New Orleans: Tulane School of Architecture, 1997.

Johnson, Jerah. *Congo Square in New Orleans.* New Orleans: Louisiana Landmarks, 1995.

Lewis, Peirce F. *New Orleans: The Making of an Urban Landscape.* Cambridge, Mass.: Ballinger Publishing Company, 1976.

Meek, A.J., and Suzanne Turner. *The Gardens of Louisiana: Places of Work and Wonder.* Baton Rouge and London: Louisiana State University Press, 1997.

Mitchell, William R., Jr., and James R. Lockhart. *Classic New Orleans.* New Orleans and Savannah: Martin-St. Martin Publishing Company, 1993.

Odenwald, Neil G., and James R. Turner. *Plants for the South: A Guide for Landscape Design.* Baton Rouge: Claitor's Publishing Division, 1980.

Odenwald, Neil G., and James R. Turner. *Southern Plants for Landscape Design.* Baton Rouge: Claitor's Publishing Division, 1996.

Ogden, Scott. *Garden Bulbs for the South.* Dallas: Taylor Publishing Company, 1994.

Seidenberg, Charlotte. *The New Orleans Garden: Gardening in the Gulf South.* Oxford: University of Mississippi Press, 1993.

Usner, Daniel H., Jr. *Indians, Settlers, & Slaves in a Frontier Exchange Economy: The Lower Mississippi Valley Before 1783.* Chapel Hill: University of North Carolina Press, 1992.

Vogt, Lloyd. *New Orleans Houses: A House-Watcher's Guide.* Gretna, La.: Pelican Publishing Company, 1985–1997.

Welch, William C. *Antique Roses for the South.* Dallas: Taylor Publishing Company, 1990.

Wilson, Samuel, Jr., Patricia Brady, and Lynn D. Adams, eds. *Queen of the South: New Orleans, 1853–1862, The Journal of Thomas K. Wharton.* New Orleans: Historic New Orleans Collection, 1999.

Brief Glossary of Plants
Commonly Seen in New Orleans Gardens

Ground Covers

Ajuga	*Ajuga reptans*
Algerian ivy	*Hedera canariensis*
Aspidistra	*Aspidistra elatior*
*Blue phlox	*Phlox divaricata*
Butterfly iris	*Dietes spp.*
Daylily	*Hemerocallis fulva*
Garden violet	*Viola odorata*
Holly leaf fern	*Crytomium falcatum*
Liriope	*Liriope muscari*
Monkey (Mondo) grass	*Ophiopogon japonicus*
Sword fern	*Nephrolepis exaltata*
Trailing lantana	*Lantana spp.*

Vines

Asian jasmine	*Trachelopsermum asiaticum*
Bougainvillea	*Bougainvillea sepctabilis*
*Carolina yellow jessamine	*Gelsemium sempervirens*
Chinese wisteria	*Wisteria sinensis*
Confederate jasmine	*Trachelospermum jasminoides*
*Coral honeysuckle	*Lonicera sempervirens*
Fig vine	*Ficus pumila*
Firecracker vine	*Manettia cordifolia*
Mandevilla	*Mandevilla splendens*
Moonflower	*Ipomoea alba*
*Morning glory	*Ipomoea purpurea*
*Passion flower (Maypop)	*Passiflora incarnata*
Rosa de montana	*Antigonon leptopus*
*Trumpet vine	*Campsis radicans*

Shrubs

Althea	*Hibiscus syriacus*
Angel's trumpet	*Brugmansia arborea*
Ardesia	*Ardisia crispa*
Aucuba	*Aucuba japonica*
Azalea	*Rhododendron indica*
Banana shrub	*Michelia figo*
Butterfly bush	*Buddleia alternifolia*
Camellia	*Camellia spp.*
Candlestick tree	*Cassia alata*
Cassia	*Cassia corymbosa; splendida*
Chinese hibiscus	*Hibiscus Rosa-sinensis*
Fatsia	*Fatsia japonica*
Gardenia	*Gardenia jasminoides*
Hydrangea	*Hydrangea macrophylla*
Kumquat	*Fortunella japonica*
Lantana	*Lantana camera*
Mahonia	*Mahonia spp.*
Nandina	*Nandina domestica*
*Oakleaf hydrangea	*Hydrangea quercifolia*
Oleander	*Nerium oleander*
Pineapple guava	*Feijoa sellowiana*
Pyracantha	*Pyracantha coccinea*
Rice paper plant	*Tetrapanax papyriferus*
Sasanqua camellia	*Camellia sasanqua*
Night blooming jessamine	*Cestrum nocturnum*
Wax leaf ligustrum	*Ligustrum japonicum*
Yesterday-today-and-tomorrow	*Brunfelsia australis*
Yucca	*Yucca spp.*

Small Trees

*Cherry laurel	*Prunus caroliniana*
Chinese parasol tree	*Frimiana simplex*
Chinese tallow tree	*Sapium sebiferum*
Crape myrtle	*Lagerstroemia indica*
Cry-baby tree	*Erythrina crista-galli*
Fig	*Ficus carica*
Frangipani	*Plumeria spp.*

Golden rain tree	*Keolreuteria bipinnata*
Japanese plum (Loquat)	*Eriobotrya japonica*
Pomegranate	*Pumica granatum*
Satsuma	*Citrus reticulata*
Saucer magnolia	*Magnolia soulangiana*
*Sweet bay magnolia	*Magnolia virginiana*
Sweet olive	*Osmanthus fragrans*
*Wax myrtle	*Myrica cerifera*

Large Trees

*Bald cypress	*Taxodium disticum*
Chinaberry	*Melia azedarach*
*Live oak	*Quercus virginiana*
*Pecan	*Carya illinoinesis*
*Red maple	*Acer rubrum*
*River birch	*Betula nigra*
*Southern magnolia	*Magnolia grandiflora*
*Sycamore	*Plantanus occidentalis*

Perennials
(or annuals that will survive mild winters)

Agapanthus	*Agapanthus africanus*
Amaryllis	*Amaryllis spp.*
Asparagus fern	*Asparagus sprengeri*
Banana	*Musa paradisiacal*
Bird-of-paradise	*Strelitzia reginae*
Bromeliad	*Aechmea spp.*
Butterfly ginger	*Hedychium coronarium*
Caladium	*Caladium hortulanum*
Canna	*Canna generalis*
*Crinum	*Crinum spp.*
Elephant's ear	*Alocasia macrorrhiza*
Four-o-clock	*Mirabilis jalapa*
Impatiens	*Impatiens wallerana*
*Louisiana iris	*Iris "Louisiana"*
Plumbago	*Plumbago auriculata*
Split leaf philodendron	*Philodendrum selloum*

*Turk's cap	*Malvaviscus arboreus*
Umbrella plant	*Cyperus alternifolius*

Roses

Cècile Brunner	
*Cherokee	*Rosa laevigata*
Cramoisi Supérieur	
Duchesse de Brabant	
Lady Banksia	*Rosa banksiae*
Louis Philippe	
Maman Cochet	
Mermaid	Hybrid Bracteata
Mrs. B. R. Cant	
Mrs. Dudley Cross	
Natchitoches Noisette	
New Dawn	
Old Blush	
Sombreuil	
Souvenir de la Malmaison	
*Swamp rose	*Rosa palustris scandens*

Palms

Cabbage palm	*Sabal palmetto*
Canary Island date palm	*Phoenix canariensis*
Chinese fan palm	*Livistona chinensis*
Cocos palm	*Butia capitata*
*Dwarf palmetto	*Sabal minor*
Mediterranean fan palm	*Chamaerops humilis*
Sago palm	*Cycas revoluta*
Windmill	*Trachycarpus fortunei*

* = native

Sources for botanical names: Neil G. Odenwald and James R. Turner. *Southern Plants for Landscape Design.* Baton Rouge: Claitor's Publishing Division, 1996; William C. Welch, *Antique Roses for the South,* 1990.

Index

About the Authors

Lake Douglas holds undergraduate and graduate degrees in landscape architecture and is presently completing a doctorate in urban studies. While assistant director for the Arts Council of New Orleans, he was responsible for creating and administering the city's public art program. He has taught at the university level and served on regional art and design review panels. His articles and reviews have appeared in popular, professional, and academic journals in America, France, and England, including *Journal of Garden History, Journal of the Society of Architectural Historians, Design Book Review, World of Interiors, Decoration Internationale, Architectural Digest, Architecture Review, Landscape Architecture Magazine, Garden Design,* and *Southern Accents.* He has written two books, *Site Perspectives* (1986) and *Hillside Gardens* (1987) and has contributed chapters to several other books, including *Frederick Law Olmsted: Old South Prophet/New South Planner* (1979); *Garden Design* (1984); and *The Oxford Companion to Gardens* (1986). His writings have been recognized with state and national awards from the American Society of Landscape Architects. Currently an arts management consultant and garden historian, he lives in New Orleans on Bayou St. John.

Jeannette Hardy has been the garden writer for *The Times-Picayune* since 1995. Her articles have also appeared in *Horticulture* magazine. Her writings center on the gardens and gardeners of New Orleans, Louisiana, and other parts of the Southeast. She lives in the New Orleans neighborhood of Faubourg St. John, near City Park.

Richard Sexton is a noted photographer of architecture, interiors, and gardens and writes about these topics as well. He is the author/photographer of *Vestiges of Grandeur: Plantation Architecture of Louisiana's River Road, Parallel Utopias: The Quest for Community,* and *The Cottage Book.* He is coauthor/photographer of *New Orleans: Elegance and Decadence* and *In the Victorian Style,* all published by Chronicle Books. His work has appeared in *Abitare, Architectural Record, Better Homes and Gardens, Classic American Homes, Garden Design, Gulliver* (De Agostini Periodici Rizzoli), *Harper's, Los Angeles Times Magazine, Louisiana Cultural Vistas, Old House Journal, Preservation, Smithsonian,* and *Southern Accents,* among other publications. He teaches photography at New Orleans Academy of Fine Arts and is represented in New Orleans by A Gallery for Fine Photography. He lives in the neighborhood of Faubourg Marigny, near the French Quarter.